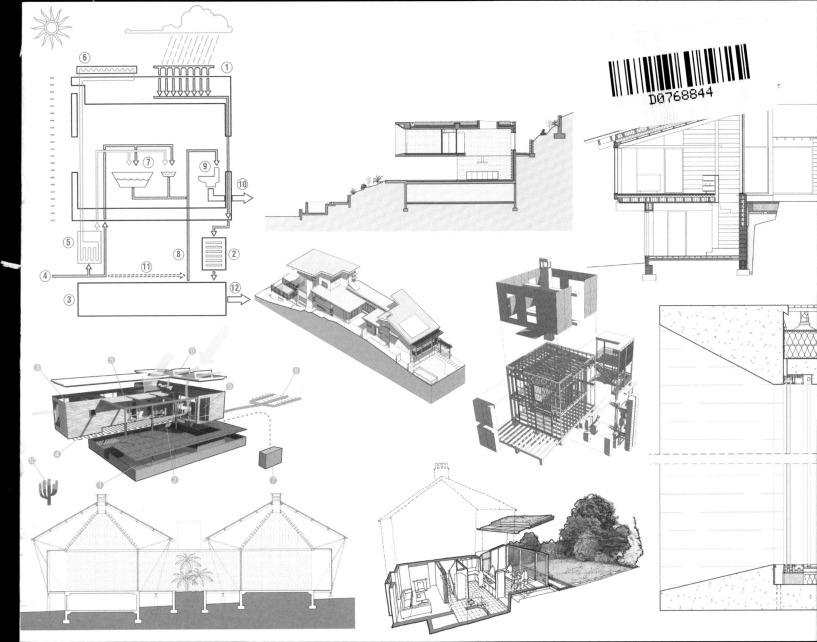

OFF GRID HOUSE PLANS

© 2020 Instituto Monsa de ediciones.

First edition in November 2020 by Monsa Publications, Gravina 43 (08930) Sant Adrià de Besós. Barcelona (Spain) T +34 93 381 00 93 www.monsa.com monsa@monsa.com

Editor and Project Director Anna Minguet
Art director Eva Minguet
(Monsa Publications)
Printing Gómez Aparicio

Shop online:
www.monsashop.com

Follow us!
Instagram: @monsapublications
Facebook: @monsashop

ISBN: 978-84-17557-26-3
D.L. B 19812-2020
November 2020

OFF GRID HOUSE PLANS

monsa

INTRO

Off-Grid House Plans has more than 250 floor plans, sections, sketches
and elevations, as well as all the construction details in all projects.
An Off-Grid system allows you to live without using a utility company,
generating your own energy. A well designed system also has numerous
environmental advantages, that help you to reduce your carbon footprint,
providing cleaner, more sustainable energy. In the long-term it is financially
viable, and also teaches us how to consume energy responsibly.

These off-grid homes, which run on solar, wind or hydro power, are just
a few examples of how people are leaving the city behind for a life in the
country in contact with nature.

Off-Grid House Plans contiene más de 250 planos de plantas, secciones,
bocetos y alzados, así como todos los detalles constructivos de los
proyectos. Un sistema Off-Grid te permite una vida independiente de una
compañía de suministros, generando tu propia energía. Además un sistema
bien diseñado también tiene múltiples ventajas medioambientales, ayudando
a reducir tu huella de carbono, y aportando una energía más limpia y
sostenible. A largo plazo es conveniente económicamente, y también nos
permite aprender a tener un consumo energético responsable.

Estos hogares fuera de la red, que funciona con energía solar, eólica o
hidroeléctrica, son solo algunos ejemplos de cómo la gente está abandonando
la vida en la ciudad, en favor de vivir en contacto con la naturaleza.

INDEX

24. DWELL HOME
28. 99K HOUSE (CORE)
34. PLACE HOMES
40. BARBAROS HOUSE
44. BERKSHIRE HOUSE
50. RONDOLINO RESIDENCE
56. XBO
58. MAISON LE CAP
62. HOUSE IN ALINGSÅS
70. LOOSE HOUSE
72. TRANSFORMER HOUSE
76. RINCON | BATES HOUSE
80. ENGLISH RESIDENCE

84. BIOCASA
88. VOLGADACHA HOUSE
94. A FOREST FOR A MOON DAZZLER
98. HILL END ECOHOUSE
104. GULLY HOUSE
106. JOANOPOLIS HOUSE
110. PASSIVE HOUSE V.W.
114. VILLA NUOTA
118. IT HOUSE
120. A'BODEGA
126. CASA TMOLO
134. GREEN.O.LA

DECALOGUE FOR A BIOCLIMATIC DESIGN AND HEALTHY HOUSE

1. The main façade may be facing the sun (to the south if we are in the Northern Hemisphere, and to the north if we are in the Southern Hemisphere). Position eaves depending on the latitude, to provide shade in summer and let sunlight through in winter.
2. Close to deciduous trees, shade in summer.
3. A gallery with large glass expanses on the sunny side of the house. It acts as solar collector.
4. Solid walls and solid materials allow greater thermal inertia, so they accumulate more heat to release later.
5. If the house has a chimney, we would recommend thermo wind self-suction hood, which evacuates the fumes, excess heat and prevents them being sucked back in.
6. Fit hinged skylights in the roof and adjustable flaps at the bottom of the face oposed to the sun. They light up hallways, bathrooms, attics and other rooms. As they fold up and can be adjusted, when opened in summer they get rid of the hot air and create cross ventilation.
7. Use natural insulation in walls and breathable waterproof sheets for roofs.
8. Use local building materials when possible.
9. The materials used must be safe regarding their radioactivity. Under no circumstances should they emit more than 180`mrad per year, or release radon gas, which is associated with certain lung cancers.
10. The home's electrical balance must be in keeping with the environmental maximum, which ranges from 120 to 300 volts per meter. For that reason synthetic materials should not be overused, or the ferromagnetic, materials generating electrostatic charges.

1. La fachada principal ha de estar orientada hacia sol (hacia el sur si estamos en el hemisferio norte y hacia el norte si estamos en el hemisferio sur). Posicionaremos aleros en función de la latitud para dar sombra en verano y dejar pasar la luz solar en invierno.
2. Situaremos en los alrededores árboles de hoja caduca para que hagan sombra en verano.
3. Una galería adosada con grandes superficies acristaladas en el lado sol de la vivienda sirve de captador solar.
4. Las paredes, muros y materiales macizos permiten una mayor inercia térmica, es decir, acumulan mejor el calor para desprenderlo horas después.
5. En caso de tener chimenea, sería recomendable rematarla con un capuchón autoaspirante termoeólico, que evacua los humos y el exceso de calor, y evita los retornos hacia el interior.
6. Disponer claraboyas abatibles en la cubierta y trampillas regulables en la parte inferior de la fachada opuesta al sol ayuda a iluminar pasillos, baños, buhardillas y otras estancias. Al ser abatibles y regulables, se pueden abrir en verano para evacuar el aire caliente y crear ventilación cruzada.
7. Usar aislamiento natural en las paredes y láminas impermeabilizantes transpirables para las cubiertas.
8. Usar materiales locales de construcción siempre que sea posible.
9. Los materiales usados deben ser inocuos radiactivamente; en ningún caso deben emitir más de 180 mrad por año, ni desprender gas radón, que está asociado a ciertos cánceres de pulmón.
10. El equilibrio eléctrico de la vivienda deberá ajustarse al máximo al ambiental, que va de los 120 a los 300 voltios por metro. Por dicho motivo no se debe abusar de materiales sintéticos, ni de los ferromagnéticos, pues generan cargas electrostáticas.

Bioclimatic design of a building

1. Summer.
2. Winter.

Diseño bioclimático de un edificio

1. Verano.
2. Invierno.

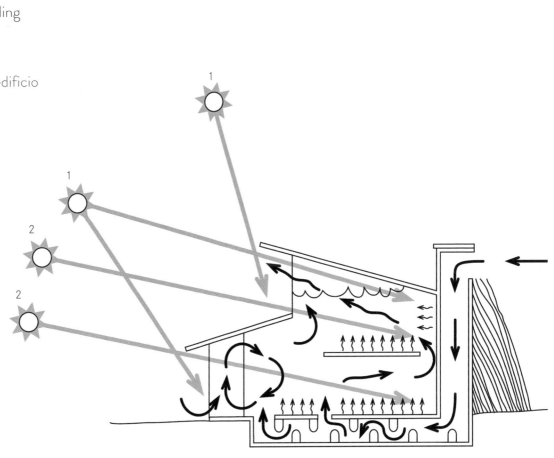

Installation of a mini wind turbine

1. Wind turbine.
2. Household power system.
3. Transformer.
4. Power output.

Instalación de un aerogenerador doméstico

1. Turbina.
2. Red de suministro eléctrico.
3. Transformador.
4. Potencia de salida.

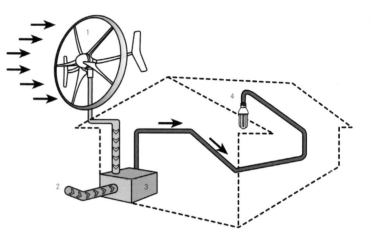

Heat recovery ventilation system

1. Solar thermal panels (optional).
2. Insulation.
3. Triple glazed low-E windows.
4. Supply air.
5. Extract air.
6. Heat recovery ventilation system.
7. Ground heat exchanger.

Sistema de ventilación con recuperación de calor

1. Placas solares térmicas (opcional).
2. Aislamiento.
3. Acristalamiento con triple vidrio.
4. Aire de entrada.
5. Aire de succión.
6. Sistema de ventilación con recuperación de calor.
7. Intercambiador de calor.

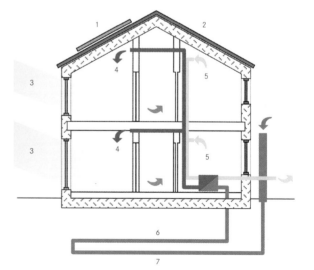

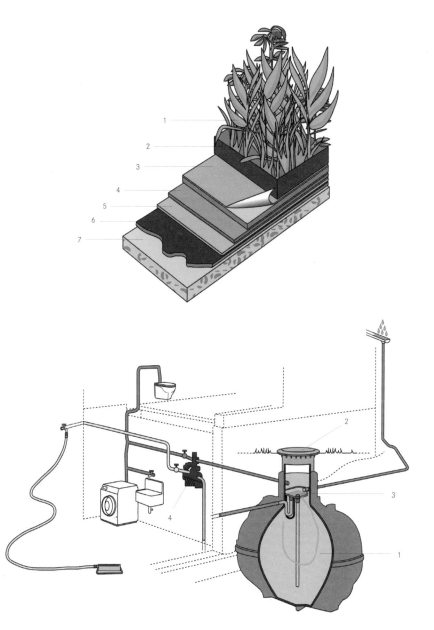

Diagram of roof garden

1. Plant cover.
2. Plant substrate.
3. Draining membrane.
4. Insulation.
5. Protective geotextile.
6. Roof membrane.
7. Structural support.

Esquema de cubierta ajardinada

1. Manto vegetal.
2. Sustrato vegetal.
3. Membrana drenante.
4. Aislante.
5. Geotejido de protección.
6. Membrana de cubierta.
7. Soporte estructural.

Rainwater collection system

1. Tank.
2. PE telescopic cover.
3. Filtration equipment.
4. Pumping device.

Sistema de recogida de aguas pluviales

1. Tanque.
2. Cubierta telescópica con tapa de PE transitable.
3. Dispositivo de filtración.
4. Dispositivo de bombeo.

TYPES OF GEOTHERMAL INSTALLATIONS

1. Surface collector: a horizontal loop is installed at a depth of between one and two meters. It requires a lot of space.
2. Geothermal probe or vertical sensor: it requires much less space in exchange for greater depth, making it ideal for urban areas and apartment blocks.
3. Geopanel: the circuit is built into prefabricated panels that are placed in trenches about three meters deep. It requires little space and is cheaper.
4. Underground water collector: underground water can also be used, as long as it not below 50 feet.
5. Soil temperature: summer 14°C, winter 14°C.
6. Ideal temperature: summer 23°C, winter 21°C.
7. Outside temperature: summer 36°C, winter 2°C.
8. Air convectors.
9. Heat pump.
10. Underfloor heating.
11. Conventional radiator.

1. Colector de superficie: un circuito horizontal se instala a una profundidad de entre uno y dos metros. Requiere mucho terreno.
2. Sonda geotérmica o captador vertical: requiere mucho menos espacio a cambio de mayor profundidad, por lo que resulta ideal para núcleos urbanos y viviendas plurifamiliares.
3. Geopanel: el circuito viene integrado en placas prefabricadas que se colocan en zanjas de unos tres metros de profundidad. Requiere poco terreno y es más económico.
4. Captador de aguas subterráneas: las aguas del subsuelo también pueden utilizarse, siempre que no estén por debajo de los quince metros.
5. Temperatura tierra: verano 14°C, invierno 14°C.
6. Temperatura confort: verano 23°C, invierno 21°C.
7. Temperatura exterior: verano 36°C, invierno 2°C.
8. Convectores de aire.
9. Bomba de calor.
10. Suelo radiante.
11. Radiador convencional.

Underfloor heating

1. Ceramics.
2. Mortar.
3. Binding for pipes.
4. Polystyrene insulation.
5. Wrought.
6. Tube circuit – the water flows through these tubes at a temperature between 34°C and 46°C.
7. The heat radiated from the floor heats the room to between 18°C and 22°C.

Calefacción por suelo radiante

1. Cerámica.
2. Mortero.
3. Malla de fijación de la tubería.
4. Aislante de poliestireno.
5. Forjado.
6. Circuito de tuberías: el agua circula por estas tuberías a una temperatura de entre 34°C y 46°C.
7. El calor irradiado desde el suelo climatiza la habitación con temperaturas de entre 18°C y 22°C.

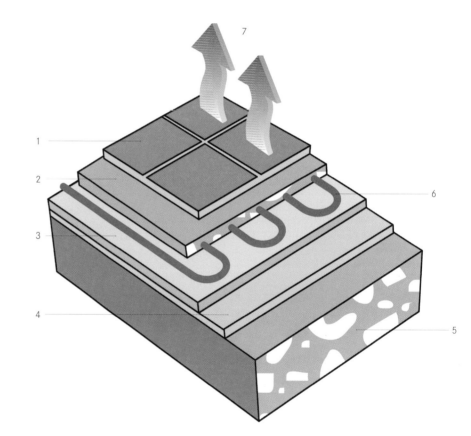

Operational diagram of a pellet stove

1. Fuel tank (pellet).
2. Cochlea for supplying fuel.
3. Gear motor.
4. Combustion burner.
5. Electrical resistance refill.
6. Vent pipe.
7. Hot air fan.
8. Hot air outlet grille.
9. Synoptic panel.
10. Centrifugal vacuum for smoke.

Esquema de funcionamiento de una estufa de pellets

1. Depósito de combustible (pellet).
2. Cóclea de alimentación de combustible.
3. Motorreductor.
4. Pebetero de combustión.
5. Cartucho de resistencia eléctrica.
6. Tubo de salida de humos.
7. Ventiladores del aire de calefacción.
8. Rejilla de salida del aire caliente.
9. Panel sinóptico.
10. Aspirador centrífugo para la descarga de humos.

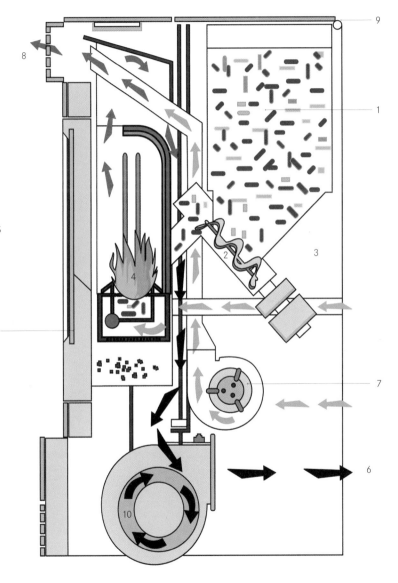

System for purification of greywater

1. Recycled water reused in garden, toilet cistern or to wash the car.
2. Process control.
3. Overflow to sewerage.
4. Water from toilet and kitchen to sewerage.
5. Greywater from bathroom and laundry.

Sistema de depuración de aguas grises

1. Agua depurada para reutilizar en el jardín, la cisterna del lavabo o para lavar el coche.
2. Control de proceso.
3. Excedente que se expulsa a la red de saneamiento.
4. Agua del inodoro y de la cocina, que se expulsa a la red de saneamiento.
5. Aguas grises del baño y la lavadora.

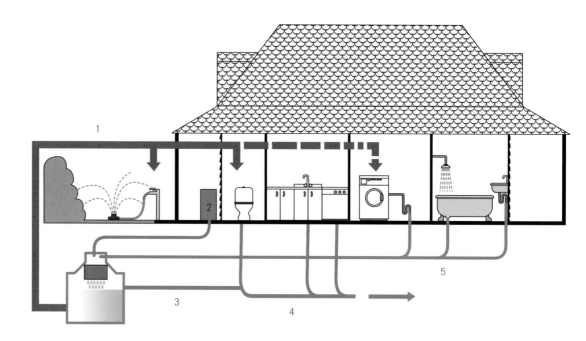

Solar thermal installation

1. Flat collector.
2. Heated area.
3. Hot water tank.
4. Washer.
5. Kitchen.
6. Bathroom.

Instalación solar térmica

1. Colector plano.
2. Espacio calefaccionado.
3. Tanque de agua caliente.
4. Lavadora.
5. Cocina.
6. Baño.

Photovoltaic solar installation

1. Regulator: protects the battery discharges and overloads, when the installation is in an isolated house.
2. Inverter: converts 12V direct current from panels to 50 Hz and 220V alternating current.
3. Meters: quantifies the electricity in the grid and electricity consumed.
4. Protection against external surges that may damage the building.
5. Batteries: only required in isolated houses, which are not connected to the grid.

Instalación solar fotovoltaica

1. Regulador: protege las baterías de descargas y sobrecargas, en caso de que la instalación esté en una vivienda aislada.
2. Inversor: transforma la corriente continua de 12V que suministran las placas a corriente alterna de 50Hz y 220V.
3. Contadores: cuantifican la electricidad vertida a la red y la consumida.
4. Protección contra sobrecargas externas que pudieran dañar la construcción.
5. Baterías: necesarias solo en viviendas aisladas que no puedan conectarse a la red.

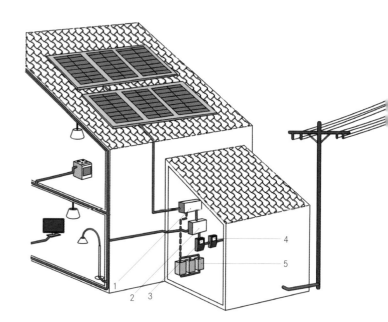

Example of installation with photovoltaic solar panels

1. Photovoltaic modules.
2. Converter.
3. Electricity for domestic consumption.
4. Counter.
5. Surplus electricity.
6. Connection to the power grid.

Ejemplo de instalación con placas solares fotovoltaicas

1. Módulos fotovoltaicos.
2. Convertidor.
3. Electricidad para consumo propio.
4. Contador.
5. Electricidad sobrante.
6. Conexión a la red de distribución eléctrica.

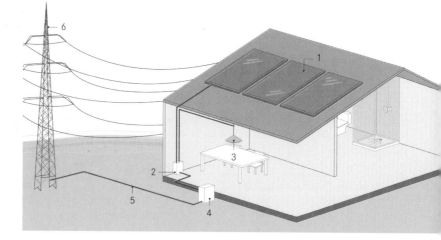

House that seeks the sun in winter and is protected from it in summer

1. The main façade and the larger windows should be in the façade receiving more hours of direct sunlight.
2. A few small windows should be in the less sunny façade, the east and the west.
3. The openings on the shady side help cooling in summer.
4. Summer sun.
5. Winter sun.

Vivienda que busca el sol en invierno y se protege de él en verano

1. La fachada principal y las ventanas de mayor tamaño deben situarse en la cara que recibe más horas de sol.
2. En las fachadas de menor insolación, la este y la oeste, han de situarse pocas ventanas y pequeñas.
3. Las aberturas de la fachada de menor insolación facilitan la refrigeración en verano.
4. Sol de verano.
5. Sol de invierno.

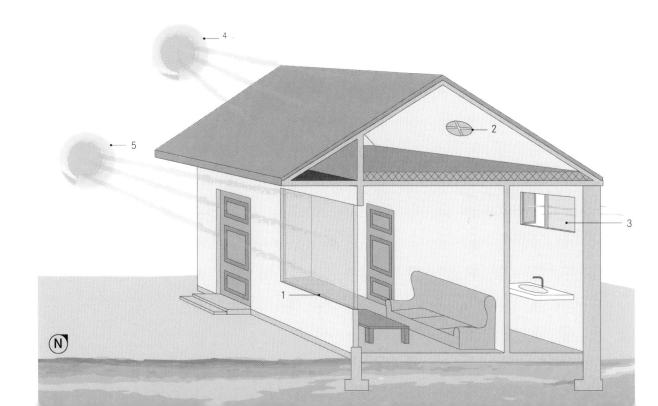

Example of installation with wind turbine

1. Wind turbine.
2. Surge controller.
3. Inverter.
4. Battery.
5. Electricity for own consumption.
6. Counter.
7. Connection to the power grid to sell the surplus energy.

Ejemplo de instalación con una turbina eólica

1. Aerogenerador.
2. Regulador de sobrevoltaje.
3. Inversor.
4. Batería.
5. Electricidad para autoconsumo.
6. Contador.
7. Conexión a la red de distribución eléctrica para vender la energía sobrante.

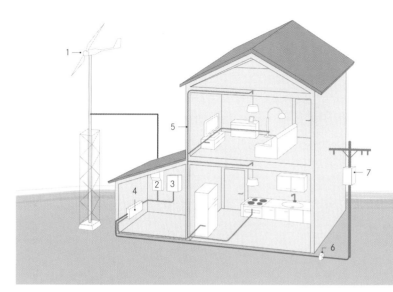

The different types of geothermal installations

1. Horizontal circuit.
2. Vertical circuit or well.
3. Exchange with ground water or surface water.
4. Heat pump.
5. Air conditioning.
6. Domestic hot water.

Las distintas tipologías de instalaciones geotérmicas

1. Circuito horizontal.
2. Circuito vertical o pozo.
3. Intercambio con aguas subterráneas o superficiales.
4. Bomba de calor.
5. Climatización.
6. Agua caliente sanitaria.

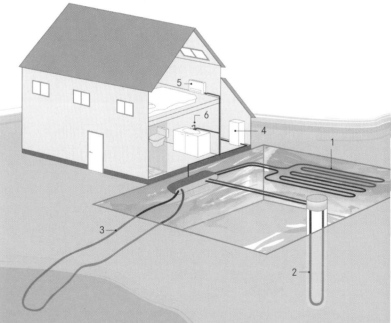

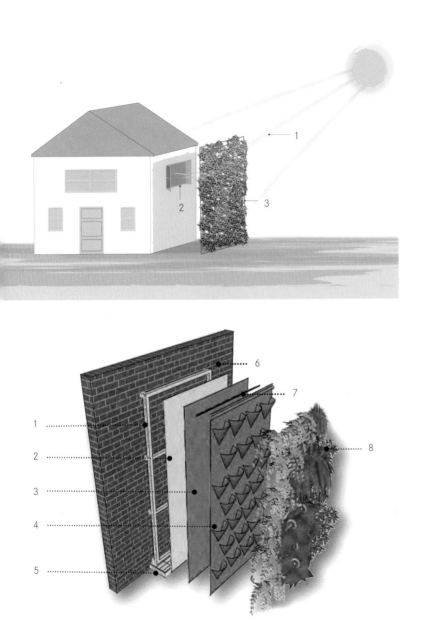

Advantages of a living wall

1. Protects from the direct heat of the sun's rays.
2. Provides a perfect shade for ventilation.
3. Insulation (reduces the transmission of heat to the dwelling).

Ventajas de la pared vegetal

1. Protección del calor directo de los rayos del sol.
2. Sombra ideal para ventilar.
3. Aislamiento (se reduce la transmisión de calor a la vivienda).

Living wall

1. Metal structure.
2. Humid insulation material.
3. Hydroponic substrate 1.
4. Hydroponic substrate 2.
5. Overflow recovery.
6. Existing wall.
7. Irrigation system.
8. Plants.

Pared vegetal

1. Estructura metálica.
2. Material aislante de humedades.
3. Sustrato hidropónico 1.
4. Sustrato hidropónico 2.
5. Canaleta de recuperación.
6. Muro existente.
7. Sistema de riego.
8. Plantas.

Room climate control

One of the clear advantages of the bioclimatic design of a home is that it can control the interior temperature naturally. When this alone is not suffice, we should use mechanical systems to provide heat or cool air. This section presents solutions for zero or low-energy consumption climate control.

Climatización de las estancias

Una de las claras ventajas del diseño bioclimático es que representa una forma de climatizar el interior de las construcciones de una manera totalmente natural. Cuando dicha solución no sea suficiente, deberíamos incorporar sistemas mecánicos de aporte de calor o frío. En este apartado presentamos soluciones de climatización de consumo energético bajo o nulo.

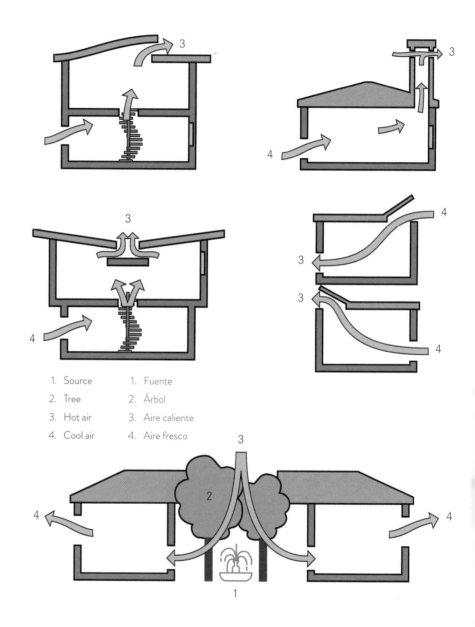

1. Source	1. Fuente
2. Tree	2. Árbol
3. Hot air	3. Aire caliente
4. Cool air	4. Aire fresco

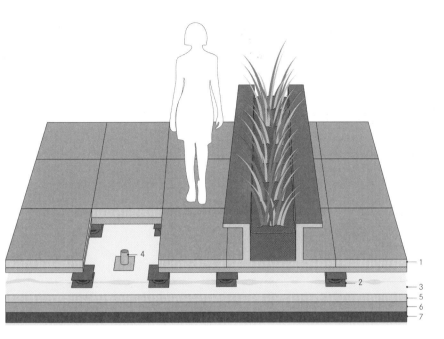

Components of a green tank roof

1. Filtration slab.
2. Adjustable support.
3. Water.
4. Overflow
5. PVC waterproof membrane
6. Hardwearing geotextile layer
7. Regulated base support

Partes de una cubierta aljibe

1. Losa filtrante.
2. Soporte regulable.
3. Agua.
4. Rebosadero.
5. Membrana impermeabilizada de PVC.
6. Capa antipunzante geotextil.
7. Soporte base regularizado.

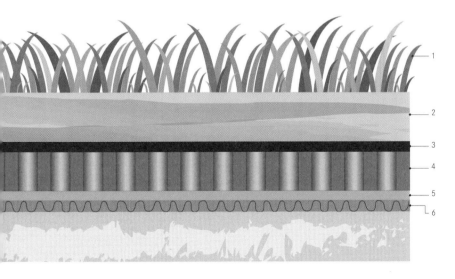

Layout of a green roof

1. Vegetation.
2. Earth or plant substrate.
3. Geotextile (fabric that prevents unwanted mixing of soils with different properties).
4. Drainage layer.
5. Anti-root barrier.
6. Waterproof membrane.

Esquema de una cubierta vegetal

1. Vegetación.
2. Tierra o sustrato vegetal.
3. Geotejido (tela que evita la mezcla indeseada de suelos con características diversas).
4. Capa de drenaje.
5. Barrera antiraíces.
6. Membrana impermeabilizante.

DWELL HOME

RESOLUTION: 4 ARCHITECTURE.
JOSEPH TANNEY, ROBERT LUNTZ
Location: Pittsboro, North Carolina, USA
Photos: © Jerry Markatos, Roger Davies, Wes Milholen
www.re4a.com

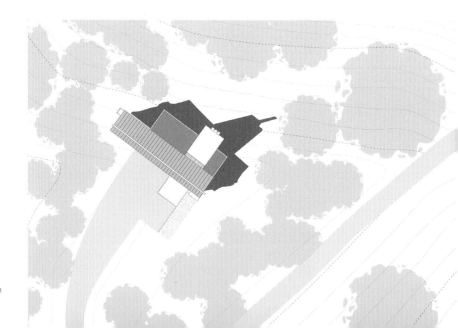

Site plan

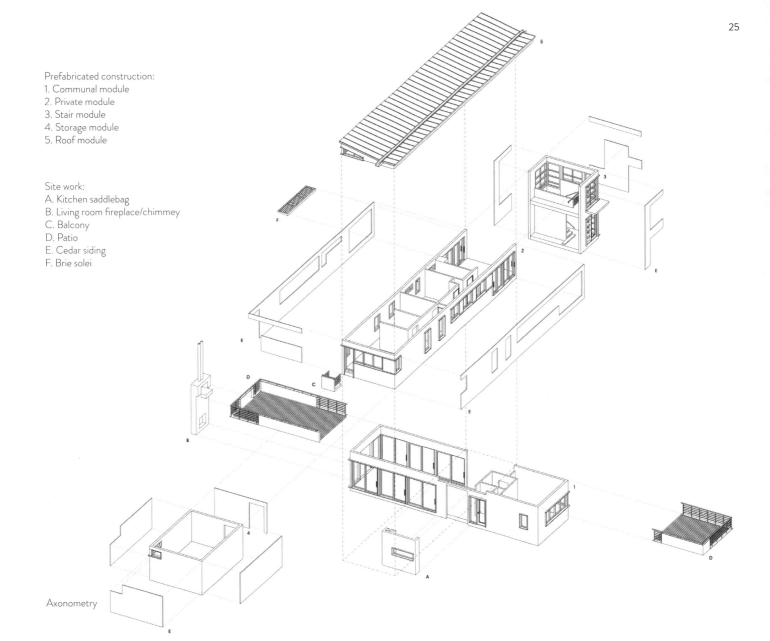

Prefabricated construction:
1. Communal module
2. Private module
3. Stair module
4. Storage module
5. Roof module

Site work:
A. Kitchen saddlebag
B. Living room fireplace/chimmey
C. Balcony
D. Patio
E. Cedar siding
F. Brie solei

Axonometry

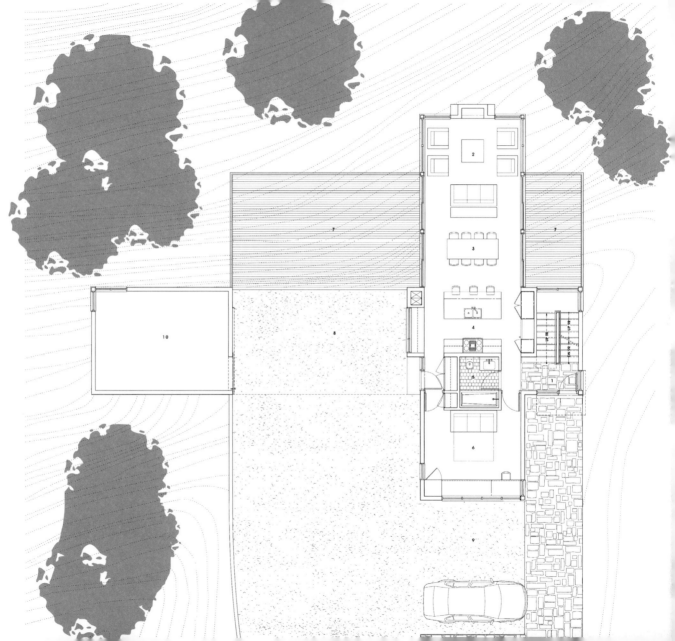

1. Main entrance
2. Living
3. Dining
4. Kitchen
5. Bathroom
6. Office / bedroom
7. Deck
8. Covered packing
9. Parking
10. Storage

First floor

1. Office
2. Bathroom
3. Bedroom
4. Master bath
5. Closet / dressing
6. Master bedroom
7. Terrace
8. Balcony

Second floor

99K HOUSE (CORE)

HYBRID ARCHITECTURE
Location: Houston, Texas, USA
Photos: © Hybrid Architecture
www.hybridarc.com

Floor plan

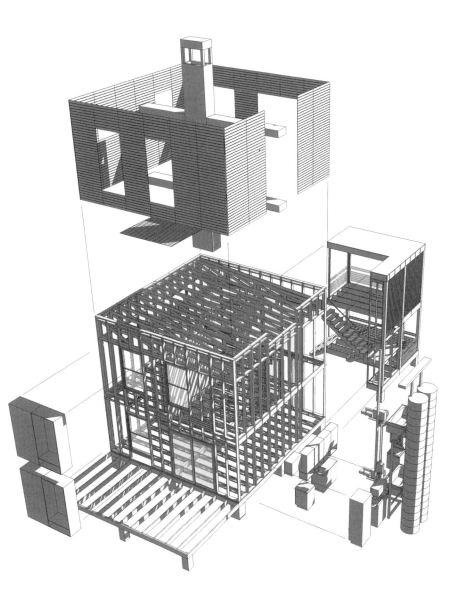

Axonometry

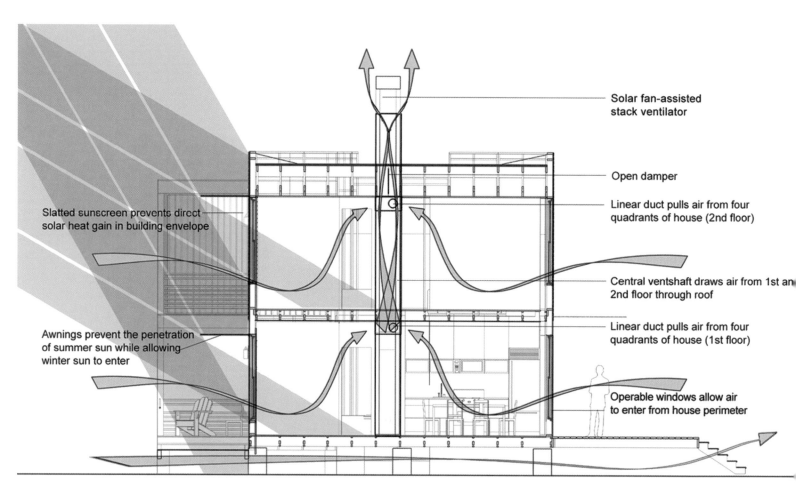

Solar fan-assisted stack ventilator

Open damper

Linear duct pulls air from four quadrants of house (2nd floor)

Central ventshaft draws air from 1st and 2nd floor through roof

Linear duct pulls air from four quadrants of house (1st floor)

Operable windows allow air to enter from house perimeter

Slatted sunscreen prevents direct solar heat gain in building envelope

Awnings prevent the penetration of summer sun while allowing winter sun to enter

Passive ventilation

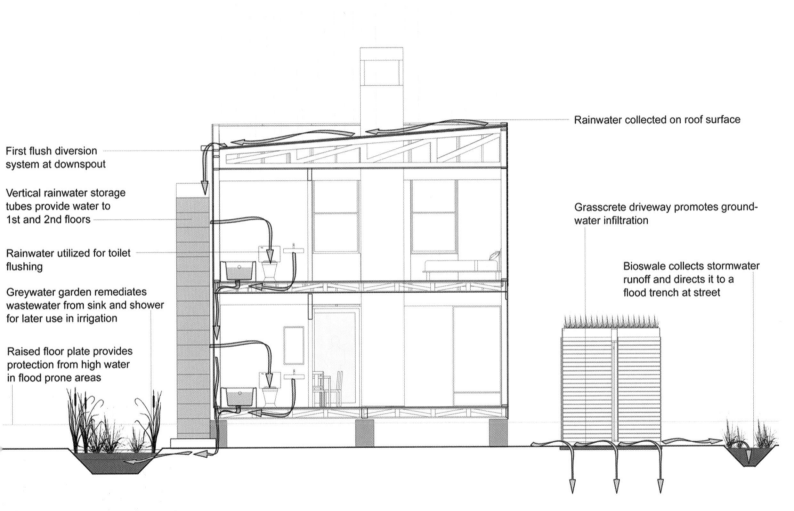

Rainwater collected on roof surface

First flush diversion
system at downspout

Vertical rainwater storage
tubes provide water to
1st and 2nd floors

Rainwater utilized for toilet
flushing

Greywater garden remediates
wastewater from sink and shower
for later use in irrigation

Raised floor plate provides
protection from high water
in flood prone areas

Grasscrete driveway promotes ground-
water infiltration

Bioswale collects stormwater
runoff and directs it to a
flood trench at street

Water management

REF

KITCHEN / DINING

LIVING

PANTRY

MECH / VENT

MOVABLE CLOSET UNITS

BATH

OFFICE / DEN / BEDROOM

W/D

UP

VERTICAL TRELLIS

PORCH

Ground floor plan

MOVABLE WALL PANELS

BEDROOM
OR DEN

BEDROOM

MOVABLE CLOSET UNITS

BATH

BEDROOM

DN

VERTICAL TRELLIS

SCREEN PORCH

First floor plan

PLACE HOMES

PLACE ARCHITECTS PLLC.
HL JOHNSTON ARCHITECT LTD.
Photos: © PLACE Architects pllc.
www.placehouses.com

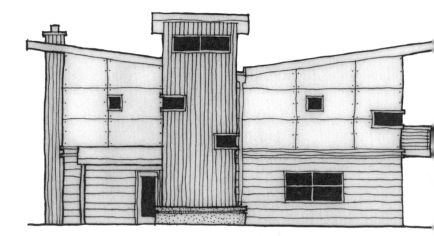

Front plan

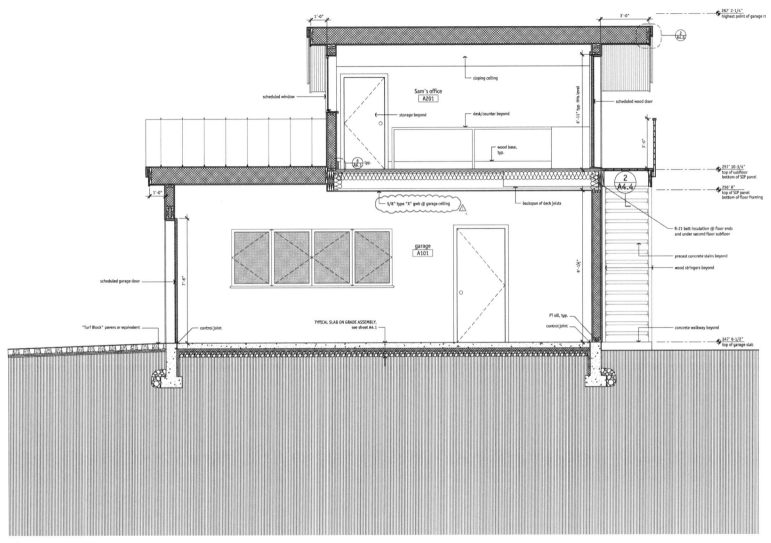

267' 2-1/4"
highest point of garage rt

257' 10-3/4"
top of subfloor
bottom of SIP panel

256' 8"
top of SIP panel
bottom of floor framing

247' 6-1/2"
top of garage slab

1'-0"

3'-0"

scheduled window

Sam's office
A201

sloping ceiling

storage beyond

desk/counter beyond

wood base,
typ.

scheduled wood door

6'-11" typ. this level

3'-0"

2
A4.4

2
A4.6

6
A6.1

typ.

5/8" type "X" gwb @ garage ceiling

backspan of deck joists

R-21 batt insulation @ floor ends
and under second floor subfloor

precast concrete stairs beyond

wood stringers beyond

garage
A101

1'-0"

7'-6"

9'-1½"

scheduled garage door

"Turf Block" pavers or equivalent

control joint

TYPICAL SLAB ON GRADE ASSEMBLY,
see sheet A4.1

PT sill, typ.

control joint

concrete walkway beyond

Accessory section

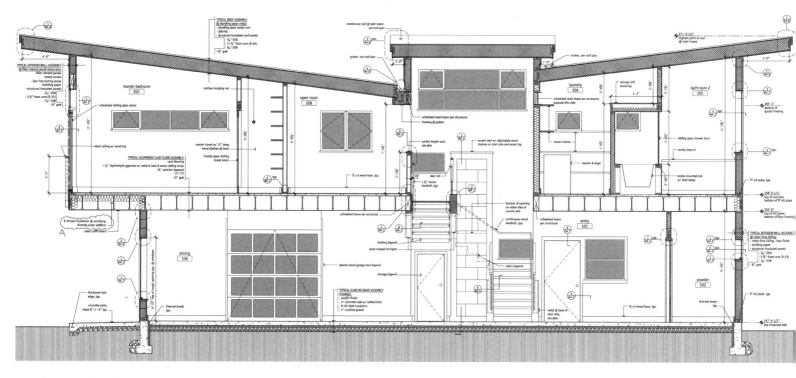

Section north-south

East elevation garage

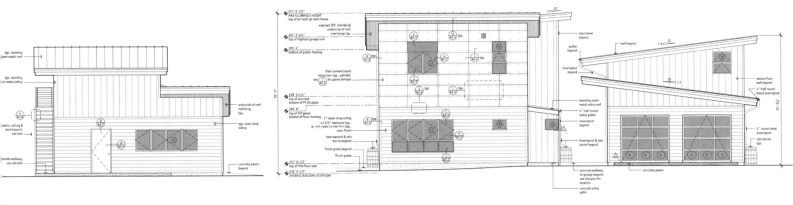

North elevation main house & garage

West elevation garage

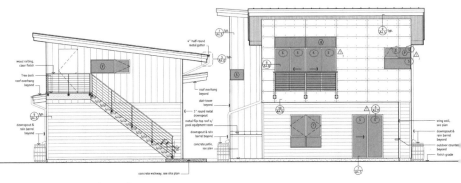

South elevation main house & garage

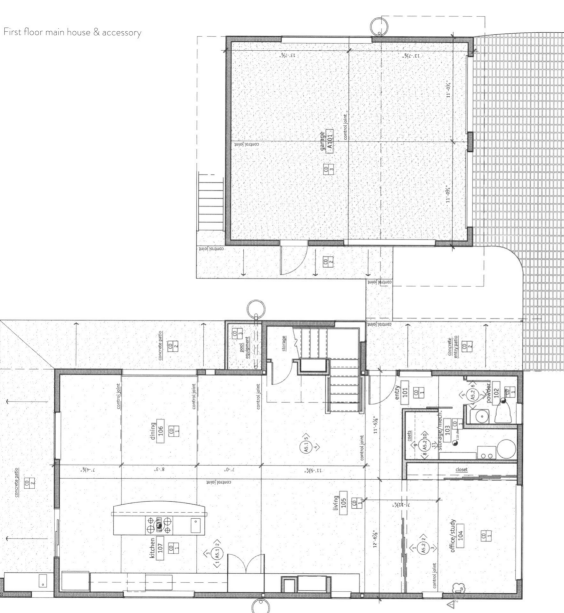

Second floor main house & accessory

sam's office
A201

master bedroom
201
CK 1

open room
208
CK 1

closet

closet

laundry
206

washer

dryer

bathroom 2
205

master bathroom
202

closet

closet

closet

closet

bedroom 4
207
CK 1

bedroom 2
203
CK 1

bedroom 3
204
CK 1

align floor tile seams with wall tile seams

tile start point

BARBAROS HOUSE

ONURCAN ÇAKIR

Location: Urla, İzmir, Turkey
Photos: © Onurcan Çakır, Ersen Corekci
www.onurcancakir.com

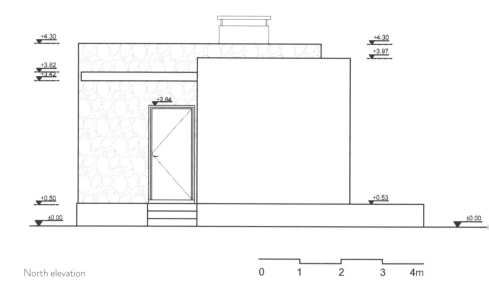

North elevation

0   1   2   3   4m

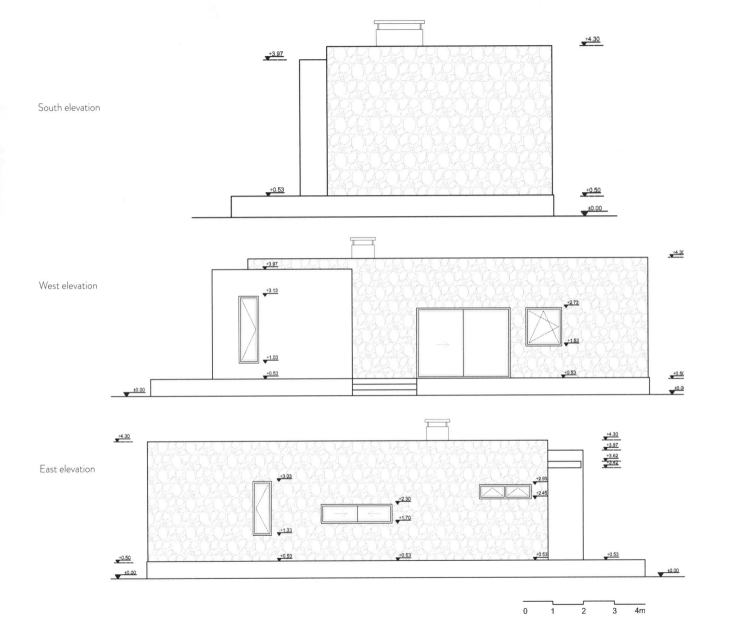

South elevation

West elevation

East elevation

0   1   2   3   4m

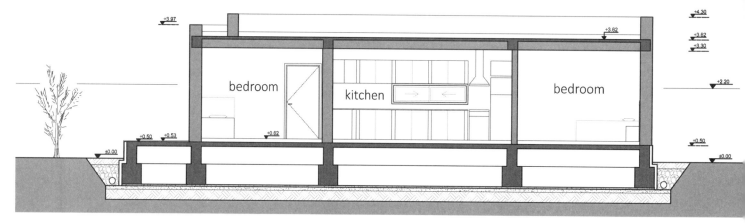

+3.97
+4.30
+3.62
+3.62
+3.30

+2.20

bedroom   kitchen   bedroom

+0.50 +0.53
+0.62
+0.50
±0.00
±0.00

Section AA

0   1   2   3   4m

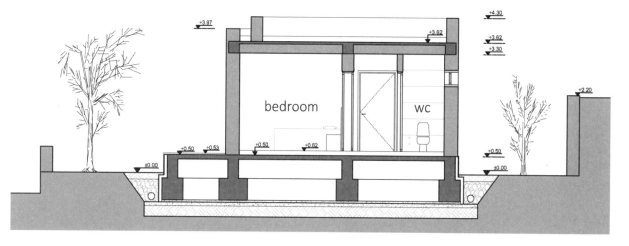

+3.97
+4.30
+3.62
+3.62
+3.30

+2.20

bedroom   WC

+0.50 +0.53   +0.50
+0.62
+0.50
±0.00
±0.00

Section BB

0   1   2   3   4m

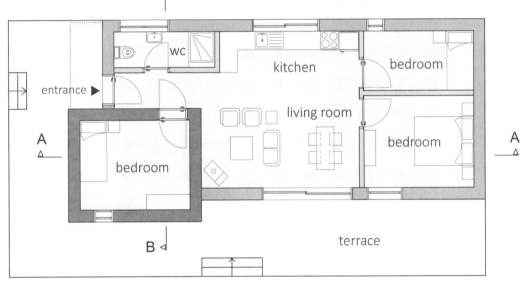

B

entrance ▶

A
A

WC

kitchen

living room

bedroom

bedroom

bedroom

B

A
A

terrace

Floor plan

N

0 1 2 3 4m

BERKSHIRE HOUSE

REVOLUTION: 4 ARCHITECTURE
JOSEPH TANNEY, ROBERT LUNTZ
Location: Palenville, New York, USA
Photos: © RES4
www.re4a.com

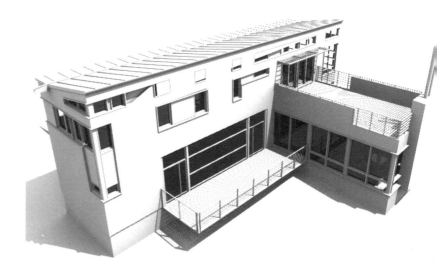

Render

East elevation

West elevation

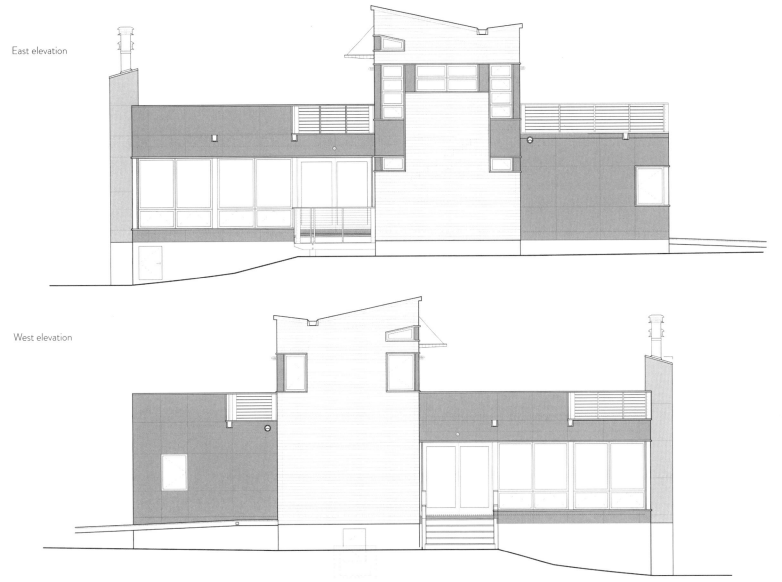

North elevation

South elevation

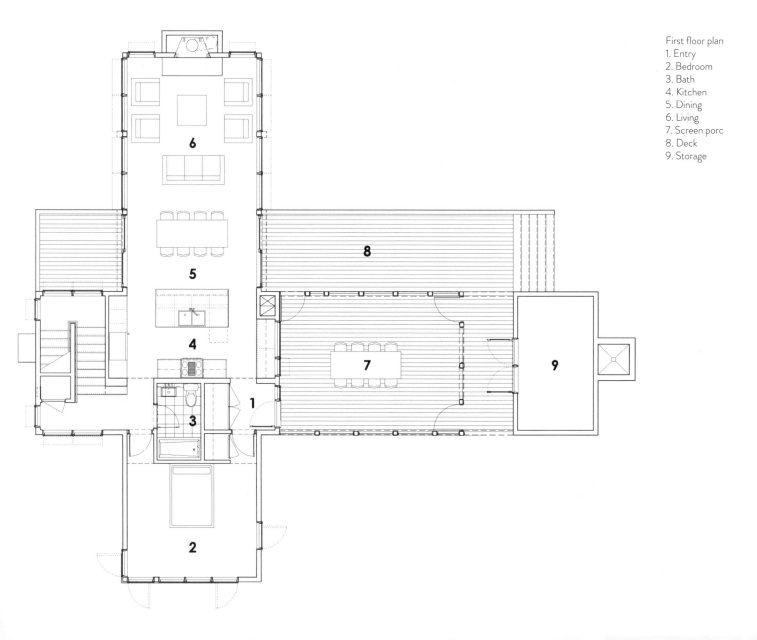

First floor plan
1. Entry
2. Bedroom
3. Bath
4. Kitchen
5. Dining
6. Living
7. Screen porc
8. Deck
9. Storage

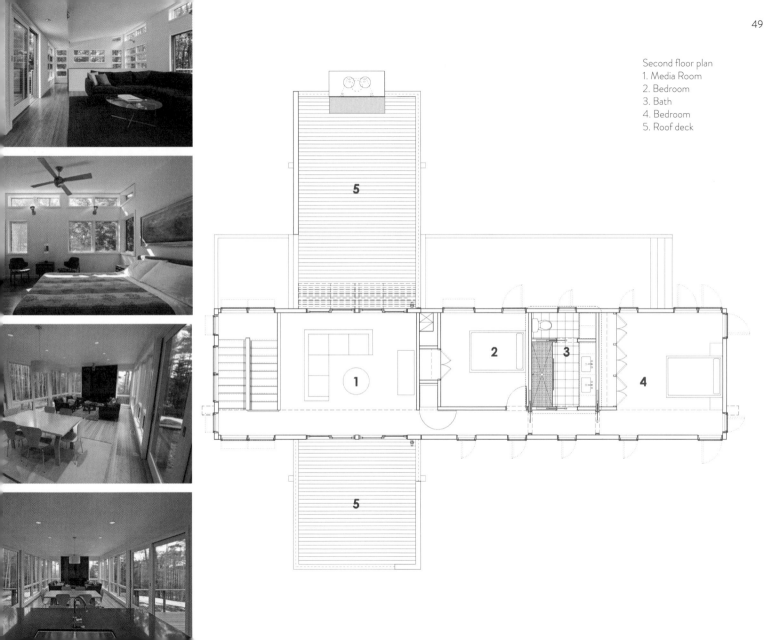

49

Second floor plan
1. Media Room
2. Bedroom
3. Bath
4. Bedroom
5. Roof deck

5

1

2

3

4

5

RONDOLINO RESIDENCE

NOTTOSCALE
Location: High Desert Near Scotty's Junction,
Nevada, USA
Photos: © Joe Fletcher Photography
www.nottoscale.com

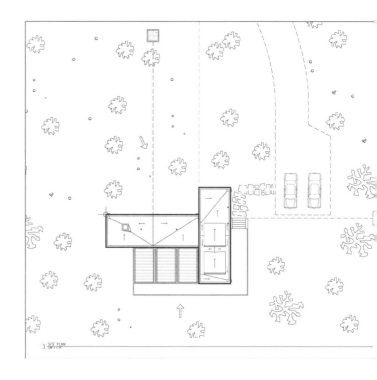

Site plan

Sustainability diagram
1. Thermal mass temperature buffer - crawlspace filled with gravel maintains even temperature year round to reduce heating and cooling needs.
2. Natural cross and stack ventilation.
3. Highly insulated Structural Insulated Panels (SIP).
4. Energy efficient hydronic radiant heating system tht can be upgraded to include radiant cooling.
5. Trellis shading system reduces solar heat gain.
6. Diffused daylighting through light monitors.
7. Off the grid local well.
8. Local septic leach field system.
9. High performance double-pane, Low-E coated windows.
10. Landscaping with local spesies that do not requiere irrigation.

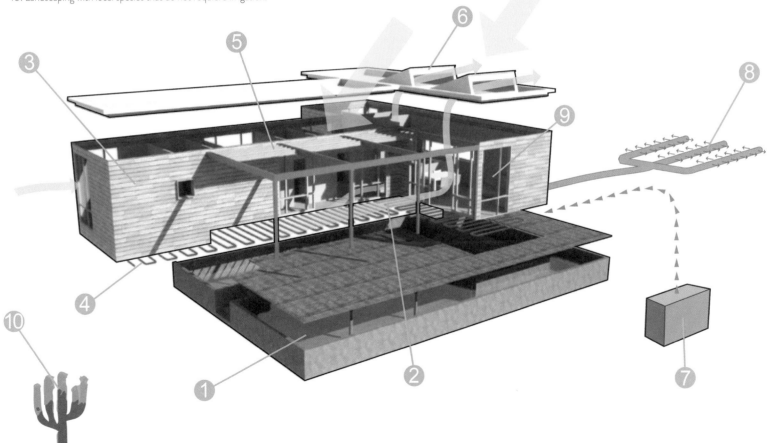

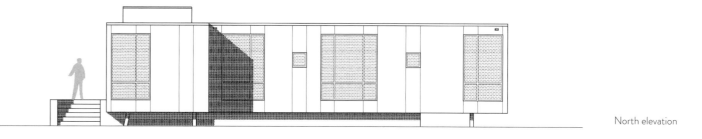

North elevation

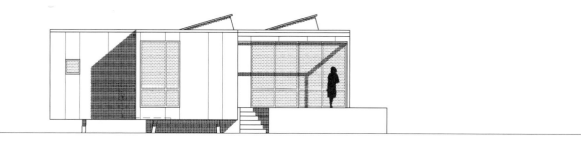

West elevation

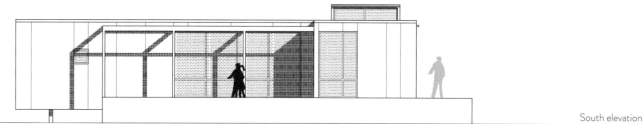

South elevation

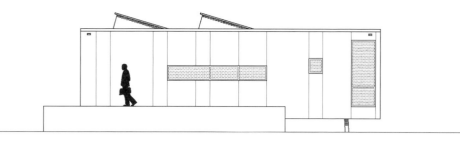

East elevation

Longitudinal section A-A

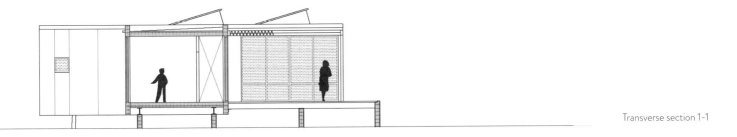

Transverse section 1-1

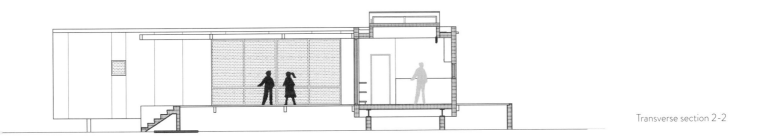

Transverse section 2-2

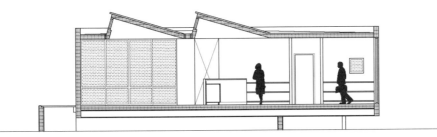

Longitudinal section B-B

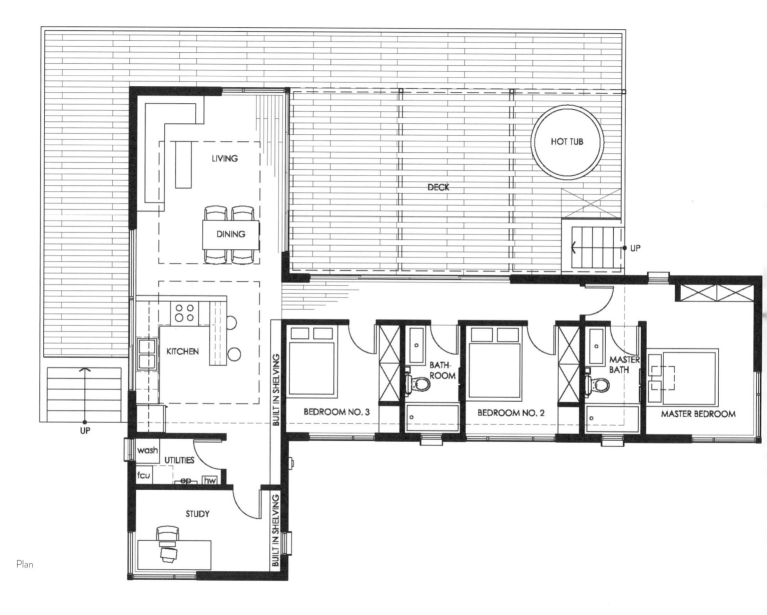

LIVING

DINING

HOT TUB

DECK

KITCHEN

UP

BUILT IN SHELVING

BEDROOM NO. 3

BATH-ROOM

BEDROOM NO. 2

MASTER BATH

MASTER BEDROOM

wash

fcu   hw

UTILITIES

BUILT IN SHELVING

STUDY

UP

Plan

XBO

70°N ARKITEKTUR
Location: Senja, Northern-Norway
Photos: © BR - Bent Raanes and Sarah Cameron Sørensen,
RSB - Rune Stoltz Bertinussen, 70N - 70°N arkitektur
www.70n.no

Plan

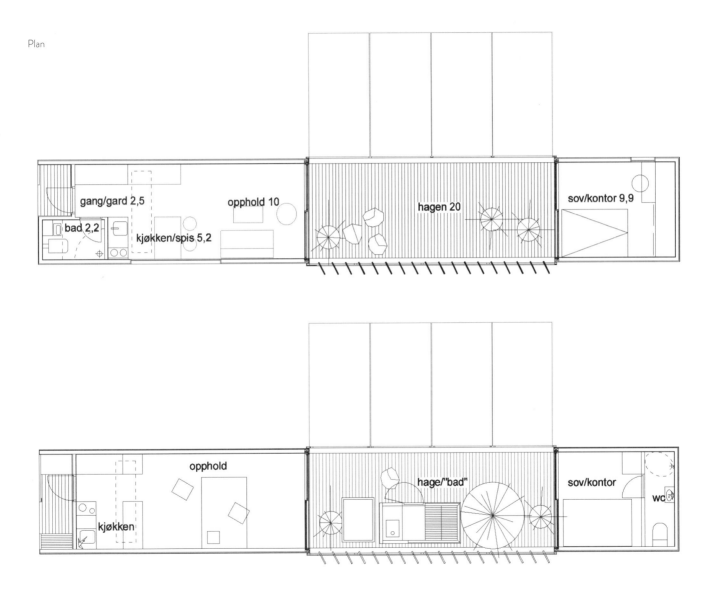

gang/gard 2,5

opphold 10

hagen 20

sov/kontor 9,9

bad 2,2

kjøkken/spis 5,2

opphold

hagen/"bad"

sov/kontor

kjøkken

wc

MAISON LE CAP

PASCAL GRASSO ARCHITECTURES

Location: Var, France

Photos: © Cyrille Weiner

www.pascalgrasso.com

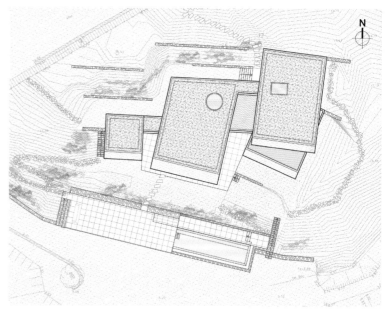

Site plan

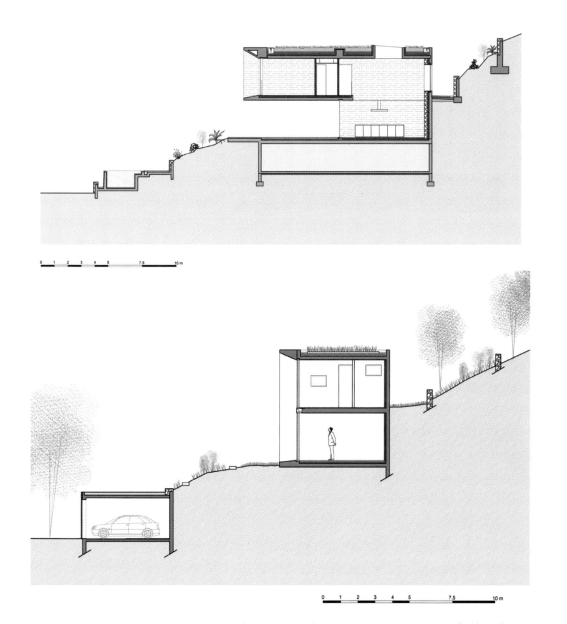

0 1 2 3 4 5   7.5   10 m

0 1 2 3 4 5   7.5   10 m

Sections

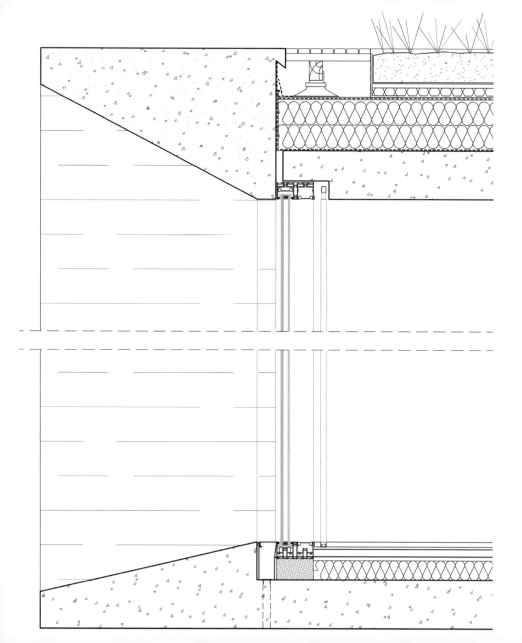

Cut detail 01

The materials chosen echo to the coast's mineral quality: raw concrete, stone, glass, stainless steel.
Poured in formworks, the bottoms of which were layered with sanded wood boards, the surface of the raw concrete retained the motif for a peculiar texture.
On the ground, in slight levitation, cantilevered, piled up.

HOUSE IN ALINGSÅS

UNIT ARKITEKTER AB
Location: Alingsås, Sweden
Photos: © Krister Engström, Unit Arkitektur
www.unitark.se

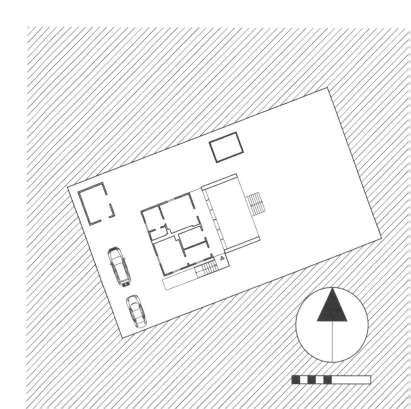

Site plan

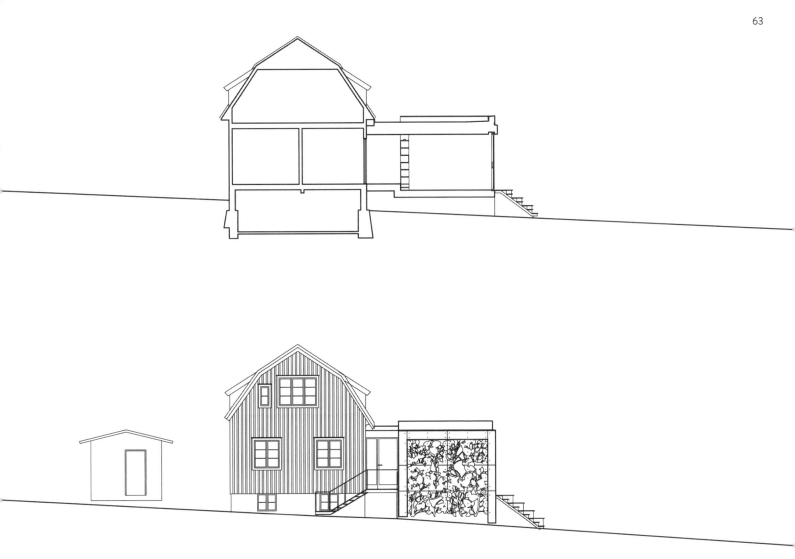

Facade sections

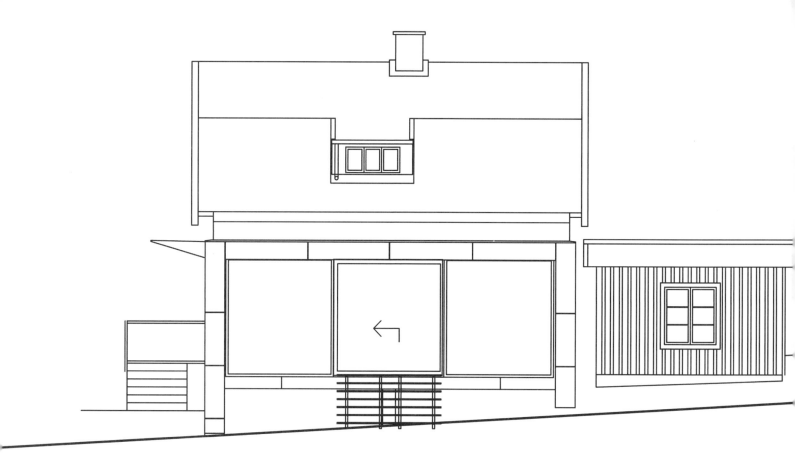

Section

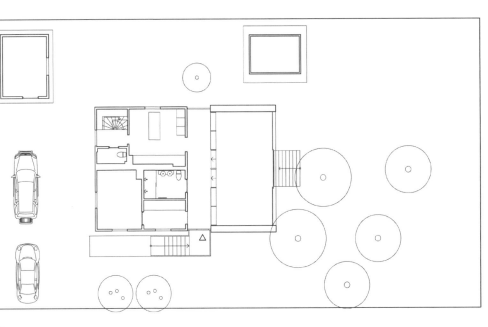

Plan

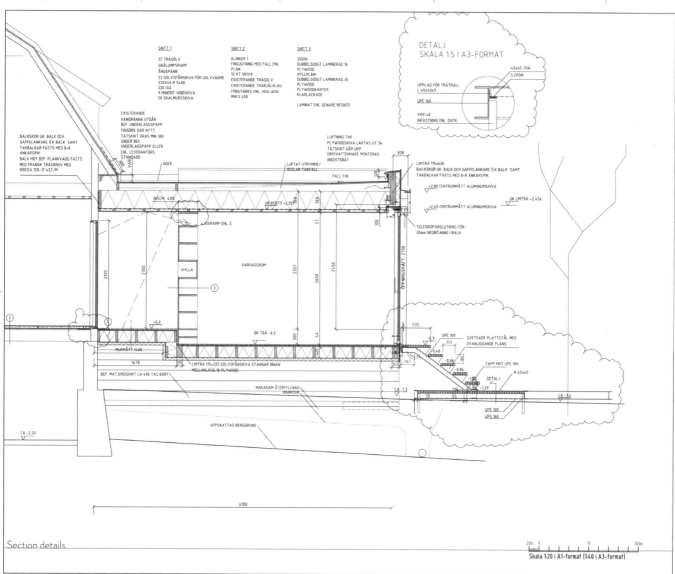

SNITT 1

22 TRÄGOLV
GRÅLUMPSPAPP
ÅNGSPÄRR
22 GOLVSPÅNSKIVA FÖR GOLVVÄRME
220X45 R S400
220 ISO
9 MINERIT VINDSKIVA
50 SKALMURSSKIVA

SNITT 2

KLINKER 1
FINGJUTNING MED FALL ENL
PLAN
12 VT SKIVA
EXISTERANDE TRÄGOLV
EXISTERANDE TRÄBJÄLKLAG
FÖRSTÄRKS ENL HUS-AMA
MIN S 400

SNITT 3

SIDOR:
DUBBELSIDIGT LAMINERAD 16
PLYWOOD.
HYLLPLAN:
DUBBELSIDIGT LAMINERAD 30
PLYWOOD
PLYWOODKANTER
KLARLACKADE

LAMINAT ENL SENARE BESKED

DETALJ
SKALA 1:5 I A3-FORMAT

45x45 TRÄ
5 EPDM

UPPLAG FÖR TRÄTRALL
L 40x40x3

UPE 160

VKR 40
INFÄSTNING ENL. ENTR.

EXISTERANDE
HÄNGRÄNNA UTGÅR
BEF. UNDERLAGSPAPP
FRIGÖRS DÄR NYTT
TÄTSKIKT DRAS MIN 300
UNDER BEF.
UNDERLAGSPAPP ELLER
ENL. LEVERANTÖRS
STANDARD

BALKSKOR UK BALK OCH
GAFFELANKARE ÖK BALK SAMT
TAKBALKAR FÄSTS MED 8-8
ANKARSPIK
BALK MOT BEF. PLANKVÄGG FÄSTS
MED FRANSK TRÄSKRUV MED
BRICKA 120-12 4ST/M

LUFTNING TAK
PLYWOODSKIVA LÄKTAS UT 34
TÄTSKIKT GÅR UPP
DRIVVATTENHAKE MONTERAS
INSEKTSNÄT

NOCK

LUFTAT UTRYMME/
REGLAR TAKFALL

FALL 1:30

LIMTRÄ 115×630
BALKSKOR UK BALK OCH GAFFELANKARE ÖK BALK SAMT
TAKBALKAR FÄSTS MED 8-8 ANKARSPIK

+2,80 CENTRUMMÅTT ALUMINIUMSKIVA

+2,40 CENTRUMMÅTT ALUMINIUMSKIVA

UK LIMTRÄ +2,456

UK KERTO +2,35

TELESKOPANSLUTNING FÖR
20mm NEDBÖJNING I BALK

NISCH 400

LJUSRAMP ENL. E

VARDAGSRUM

HYLLA

3

2

+0,0

ÖK TRÄ -0,3

SVETSADE PLATTSTÅL MED
OVANLIGGANDE PLÅS

UPE 100

TAPP MOT UPE 100

R 45x45

DETALJ

MURMÅTT 1400

LIMTRÄ 115×225 GOLVSPÅNSKIVA STANNAR INNAN
MELLANLÄGG 16 PLYWOOD

BEF. MATJORDSKIKT CA 400 TAS BORT

MAKADAM ÅTERFYLLNAD
MARKDUK

UPE 100
UPE 160

CA -2,20

UPPSKATTAD BERGGRUND

6100

Section details

20dm 0   10   20dm

Skala 1:20 i A1-format (1:40 i A3-format)

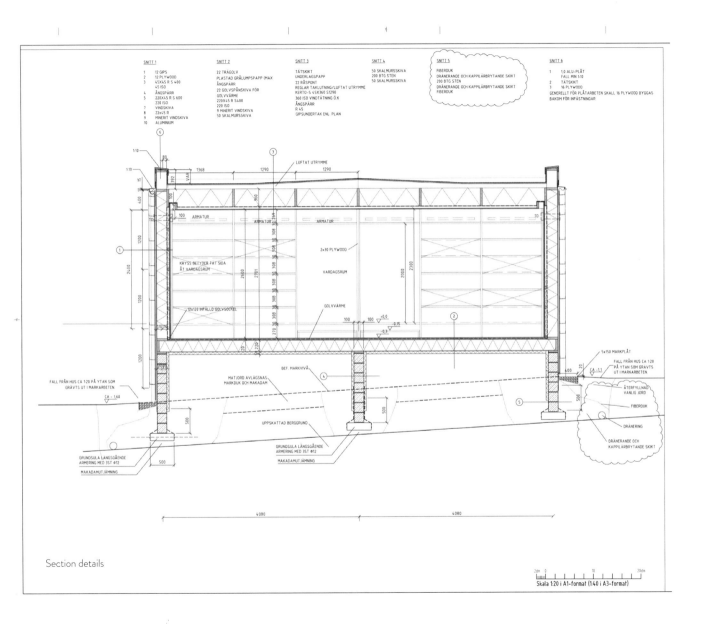

SNITT 1
1 12 GIPS
2 12 PLYWOOD
3 45X45 R S 400
   45 ISO
4 ÅNGSPARR
5 220X45 R S 600
   220 ISO
7 VINDSKIVA
8 22X45 R
9 MINERIT VINDSKIVA
10 ALUMINIUM

SNITT 2
22 TRÄGOLV
PLASTAD GRÅLUMPSPAPP (MAX
ÅNGSPARR
45X45 SPÄNSKIVA FÖR
GOLVVÄRME
220X45 R S400
220 ISO
9 MINERIT VINDSKIVA
50 SKALMURSSKIVA

SNITT 3
TÄTSKIKT
UNDERLAGSPAPP
22 RÅSPONT
REGLAR TAKLUTNING/LUFTAT UTRYMME
KERTO-S 45X360 S1290
360 ISO VINDTÄTNING Ö.K
ÅNGSPARR
R 45
GIPSUNDERTAK ENL. PLAN

SNITT 4
50 SKALMURSSKIVA
200 BTG STEN
50 SKALMURSSKIVA

SNITT 5
FIBERDUK
DRÄNERANDE OCH KAPPILÄRBRYTANDE SKIKT
200 BTG STEN
DRÄNERANDE OCH KAPPILÄRBRYTANDE SKIKT
FIBERDUK

SNITT 6
1 1.0 ALU-PLÅT
   FALL MIN 1:10
2 TÄTSKIKT
3 16 PLYWOOD
GENERELLT FÖR PLÅTARBETEN SKALL 16 PLYWOOD BYGGAS
BAKOM FÖR INFÄSTNINGAR

Section details

Skala 1:20 i A1-format (1:40 i A3-format)

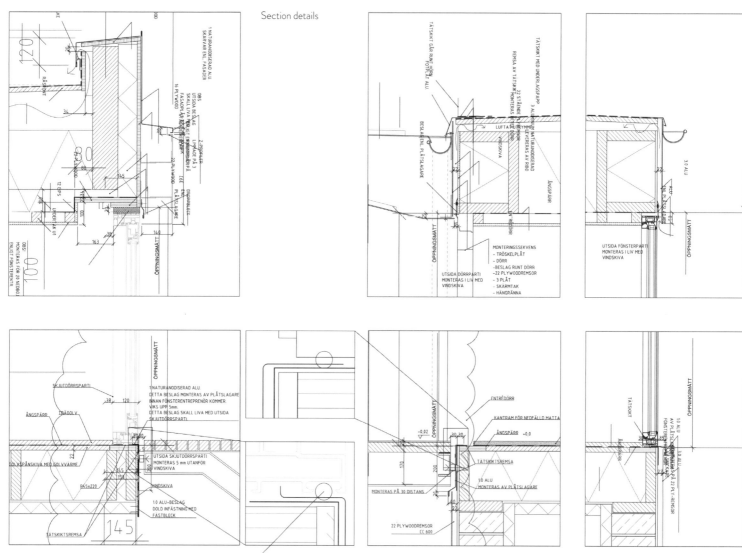

Section details

V-DETALJER SKJUTDÖRRSPARTI V-DETALJER ENTRÉDÖRR V-DETALJER FÖNSTER

Section details

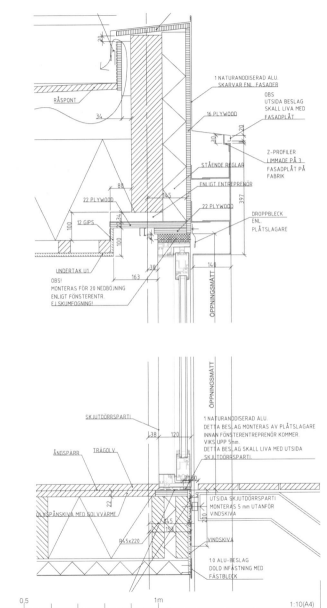

RÅSPONT

34

1 NATURANODISERAD ALU.
SKARVAR ENL. FASADER

OBS
UTSIDA BESLAG
SKALL LIVA MED
FASADPLÅT

16 PLYWOOD

Z-PROFILER
LIMMADE PÅ 3
FASADPLÅT PÅ
FABRIK

STÅENDE REGLAR

ENLIGT ENTREPRENÖR

145

22 PLYWOOD

80

22 PLYWOOD

397

DROPPBLECK
ENL.
PLÅTSLAGARE

100

12 GIPS

100

163

39

140

UNDERTAK U1
OBS!
MONTERAS FÖR 20 NEDBÖJNING
ENLIGT FÖNSTERENTR.
EJ SKUMFOGNING!

OPPNINGSMATT

DETAIL 1:10 (A4)

OPPNINGSMATT

SKJUTDÖRRSPARTI

1 NATURANODISERAD ALU.
DETTA BESLAG MONTERAS AV PLÅTSLAGARE
INNAN FÖNSTERENTREPRENÖR KOMMER.
VIKS UPP 5mm.
DETTA BESLAG SKALL LIVA MED UTSIDA
SKJUTDÖRRSPARTI.

38

120

ÅNGSPÄRR

TRÄGOLV

UTSIDA SKJUTDÖRRSPARTI
MONTERAS 5 mm UTANFÖR
VINDSKIVA

SPÅNSKIVA MED GOLVVÄRME

22

R45x220

VINDSKIVA

10 ALU-BESLAG
DOLD INFÄSTNING MED
FASTBLECK

DETAIL 1:10 (A4)

0,5

1m

1:10 (A4)

LOOSE HOUSE

LEVITATE

Location: Richmond, London, UK

Photos: © Levitate

www.levitate.uk.com

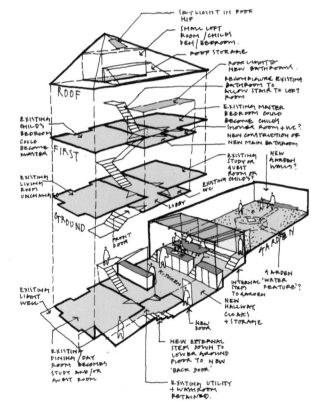

Sketch

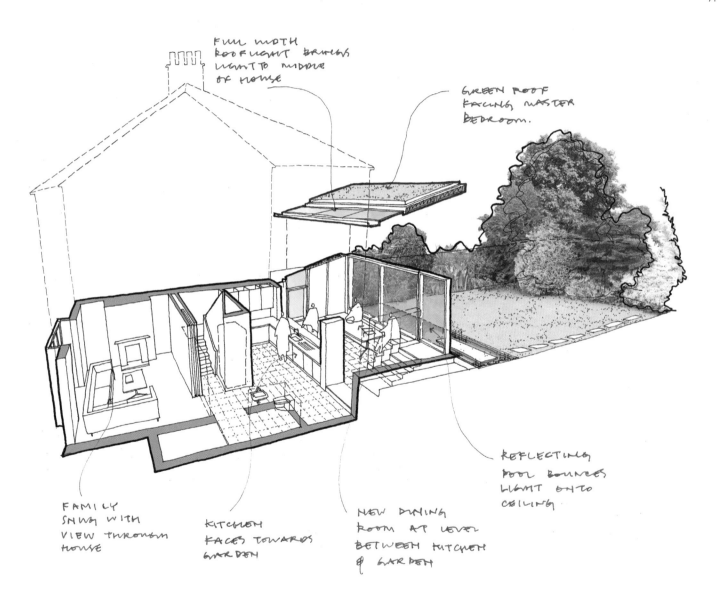

FULL WIDTH
ROOFLIGHT BRINGS
LIGHT TO MIDDLE
OF HOUSE

GREEN ROOF
FACING MASTER
BEDROOM.

REFLECTING
POOL BOUNCES
LIGHT ONTO
CEILING

FAMILY
SNUG WITH
VIEW THROUGH
HOUSE

KITCHEN
FACES TOWARDS
GARDEN

NEW DINING
ROOM AT LEVEL
BETWEEN KITCHEN
& GARDEN

Sketch

TRANSFORMER HOUSE

BREATHE ARCHITECTURE
Location: Melbourne, Australia
Photos: © Andrew Wutke
www.brathe.com.au

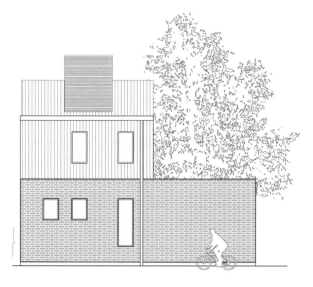

East elevation

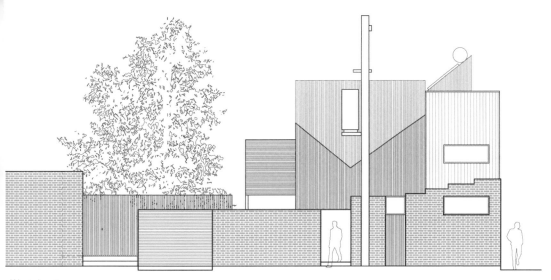

West elevation

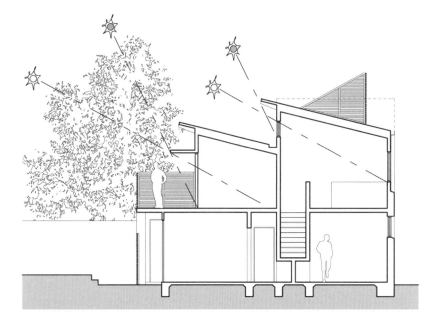

Section

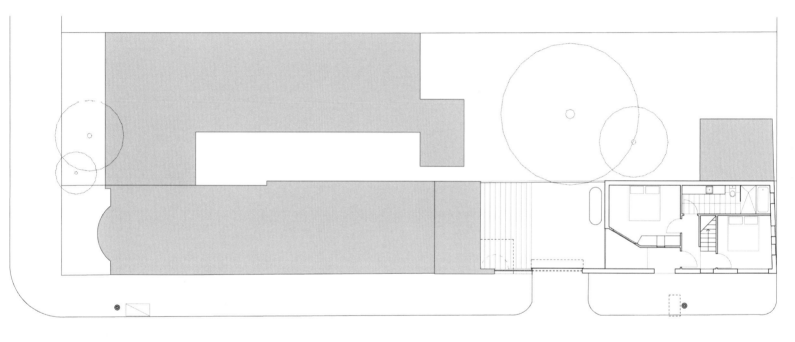

0 1 2 3 4 5

Ground floor plan

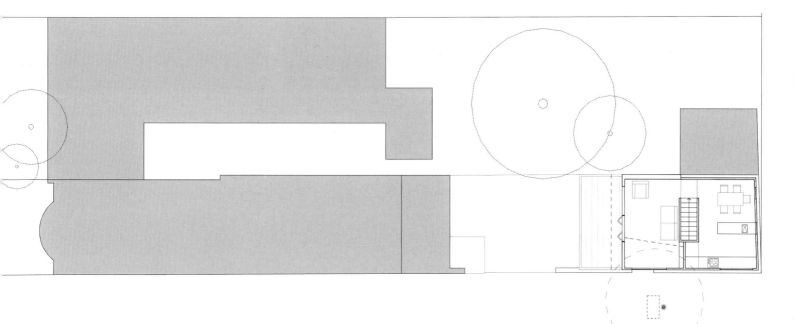

first floor plan

RINCON | BATES HOUSE

STUDIO 27 ARCHITECTURE

Architects: John K. Burke, AIA Principal; Chris DeHenzel / Hans Kuhn, Design Team
Location: Washington DC, USA
Photos: © Anice Hoachlander / Allan Russ (Hoachlander & Davis Photography)
www.studio27arch.com

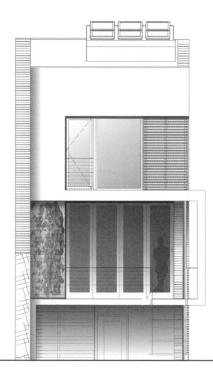

Section

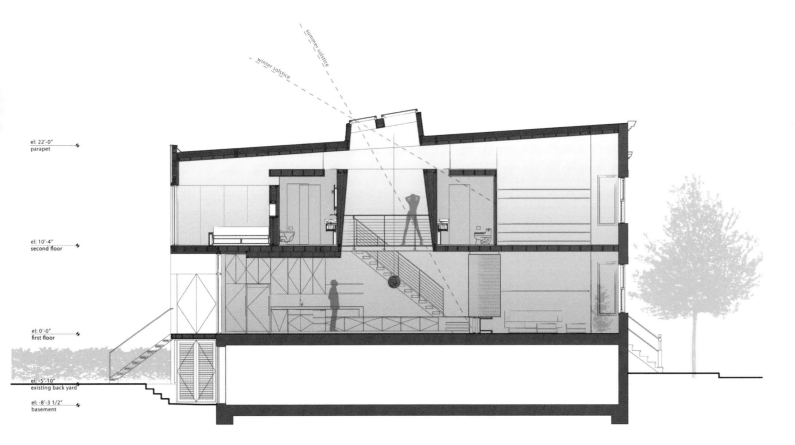

el: 22'-0"
parapet

el: 10'-4"
second floor

el: 0'-0"
first floor

el: -5'-10"
existing back yard

el: -8'-3 1/2"
basement

winter solstice

summer solstice

Section and floors

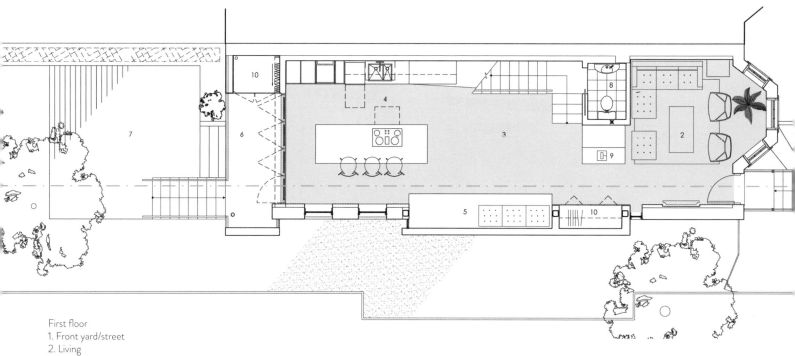

First floor
1. Front yard/street
2. Living
3. Dining
4. Kitchen
5. Bench
6. Deck
7. Back yard
8. Powder room
9. Fire place

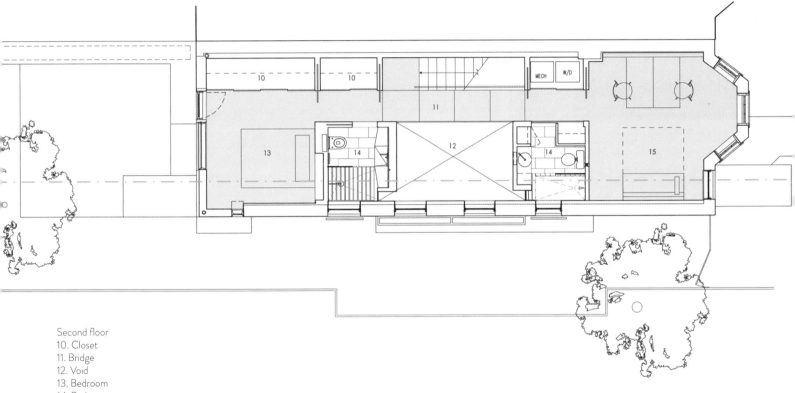

Second floor
10. Closet
11. Bridge
12. Void
13. Bedroom
14. Bathroom
15. Office

ENGLISH RESIDENCE

ZEROENERGY DESIGN (ZED)
Location: Orleans, Cape Cod, MA, USA
Photos: © Michael J. Lee
www.zeroenergy.com

1. Green Roof: The green roof is a rooftop garden that features hardy, local plants. Situated a the edge of the roof deck, it draws visitors out of the 2nd floor to enjoy the outdoor space.
2. Reclaimed Wood: Wood from the previous home was reused as a platform beneath the green roof.
3. The decking is Garapa certified by the Forest Stewardship Council (FSC).
4. Roof Deck: The second floor roof deck provides a wonderful space to take in the lake view bird watch and relax with friends.
5. Glass Handrail: A glass handrail meets the safety code but does not obscure the view for a seated person.
6. Window overhang: ZED developed the form of the house to properly shade the south-facing glass so that it blocks heat in the summer and admits it in the winter.
7. Roof and Wall insultation: The walls and roof are filled with spray foam insulation, creating an air-tight construction. Rigid insulation is also installed to prevent heat loss through wall studs, a process known as thermal bridging.
8. Solar Panels: Solar electric panels rest atop the roof and will generate 30% of the home's electricity. The home is also pre-plumbed for solar thermal hot water for when the owners eventually occupy the home year-round.

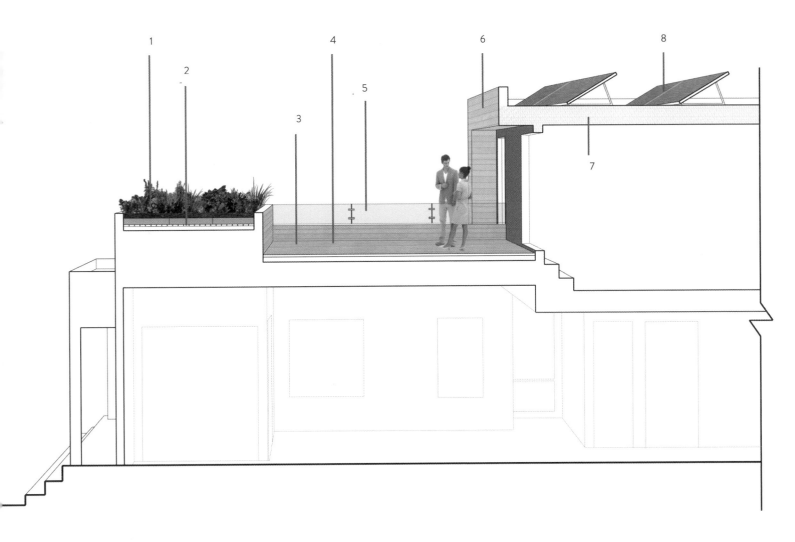

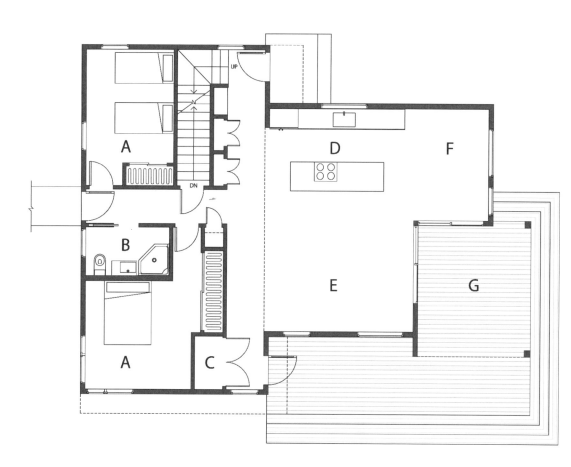

Lower floor plan
A. Bedroom
B. Bath
C. Laundry
D. Kitchen
E. Living
F. Dining
G. Covered Porch

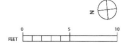

Upper floor plan
H. TV Room
I. Study
J. Master Bath
K. Master Bedroom
L. Roof Deck
M. Green Roof
N. Outdoor Kitchen

BIOCASA

LUIGI CORATO & LUCIA CAZZANINGA

Location: Brugheiro, Monza, Italy

Photos: © Luigi Corato, Lucia Cazzaniga

www.2lcarch.it

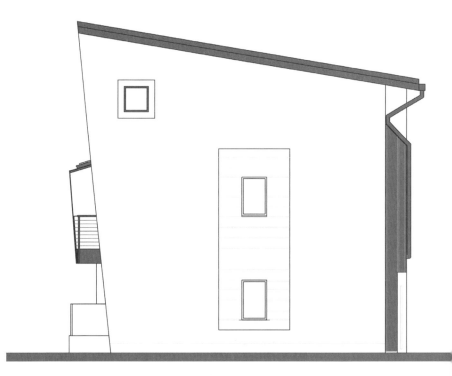

East elevation

South elevation

North elevation

Ground floor plan

First floor plan

N

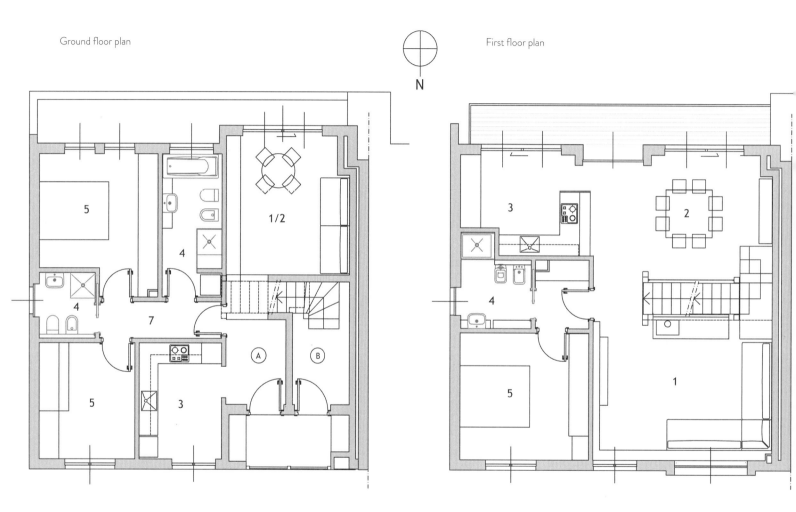

Roof floor plan

Second floor plan

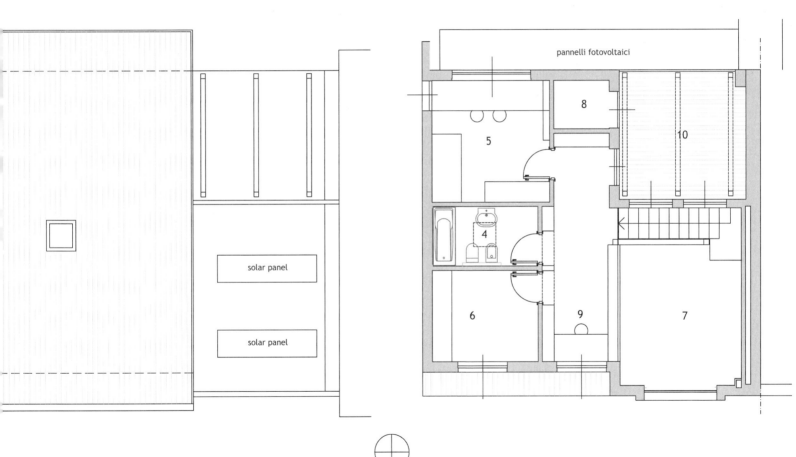

solar panel

solar panel

pannelli fotovoltaici

N

VOLGADACHA HOUSE

BERNASKONI ARCHITECTURE BUREAU

Location: Moscow, Russia
Photos: © Vlad Efimov, Oleg Dyachenko
www.bernaskoni.com

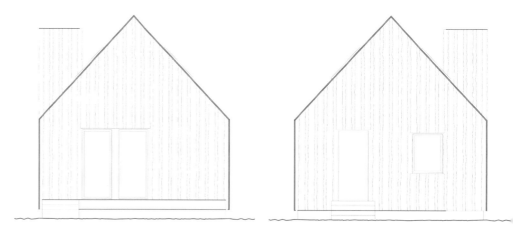

Elevations

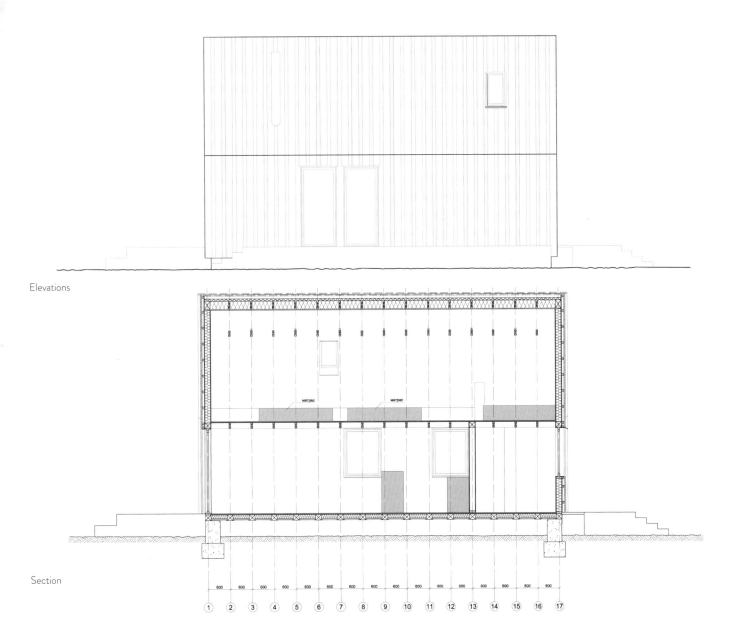

Elevations

Section

матрас матрас

① ② ③ ④ ⑤ ⑥ ⑦ ⑧ ⑨ ⑩ ⑪ ⑫ ⑬ ⑭ ⑮ ⑯ ⑰

600 600 600 600 600 600 600 600 600 600 600 600 600 600 600 600

Wood frame construction.

150 mm insulation between OSB board (walls).

200 mm insulation (floor and roof).

Total floor area.

90 sq.m

Terrace area.

90 sq.m

Footprint.

148.2 sq.m

OSB board 15 mm (walls), 18 mm (floors).

Concrete heated floors (Ensto), first floor, loft - carpet over OSB board.

Paints Tikkurila, Dulux.

Skylights Velux.

Bathroom and kitchen fixtures by Dornbracht.

Chairs by Vitra (design Charles and Ray Eames), arm chair Facett by Ligne Roset (designed by Bouroullec), floor lamp Ligne Roset.

Ceiling lighting by Ikea and some florescent lamps from the local store.

Kitchen Island and staircase: custom made of welded

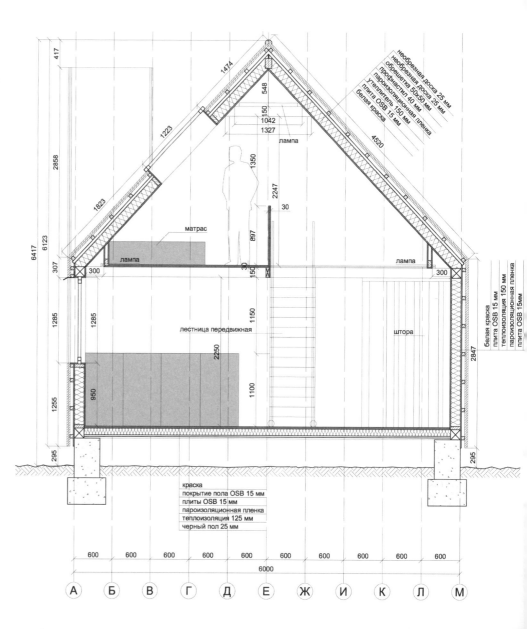

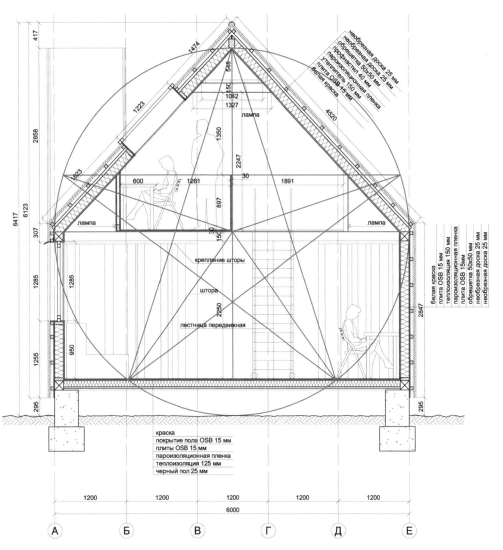

необрезная доска 25 мм
обрешетка 50х50 мм
профнастил 40 мм
пароизоляционная пленка
Утеплитель 150 мм
плита OSB 15 мм
белая краска

Белая краска
плита OSB 15 мм
теплоизоляция 150 мм
пароизоляционная пленка
плита OSB 15мм
обрешетка 50х50 мм
необрезная доска 25 мм
необрезная доска 25 мм

лампа

лампа

лампа

лампа

крепление шторы

штора

лестница передвижная

краска
покрытие пола OSB 15 мм
плиты OSB 15 мм
пароизоляционная пленка
теплоизоляция 125 мм
черный пол 25 мм

417
2858
6123
6417
307
1285
1285
1255
295
1823
1350
2247
897
600
1261
30
1891
150
1285
2250
950
295

1474
548
150
1042
1327
4520

1200 1200 1200 1200 1200
6000

А Б В Г Д Е

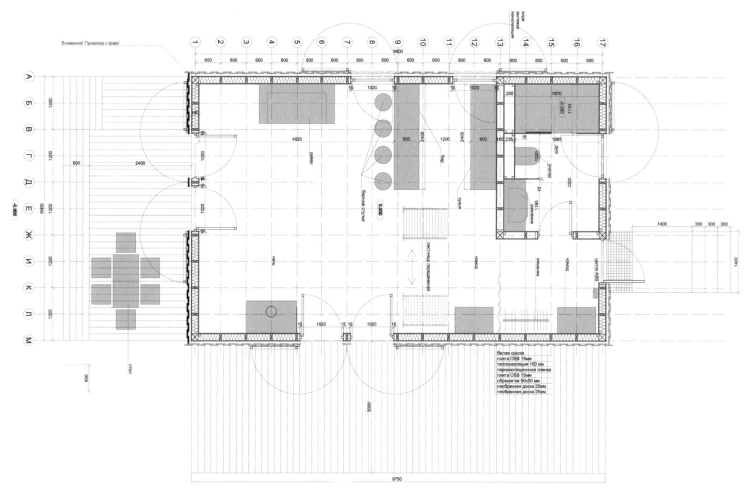

Ground floor

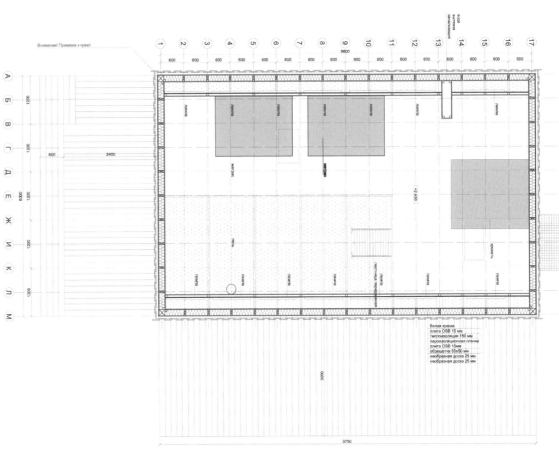

First floor

A FOREST FOR A MOON

BENJAMIN GARCIA SAXE

Location: Guanacaste, Costa Rica
Photos: © Benjamin Garcia Saxe, Andres Garcia Lachner, Isabel Amador
www.studiosaxe.com

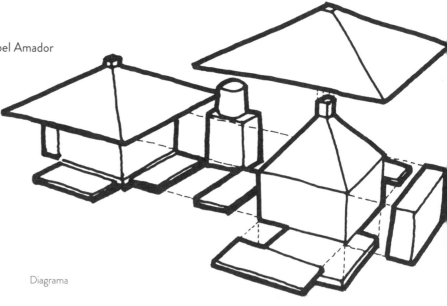

Diagrama

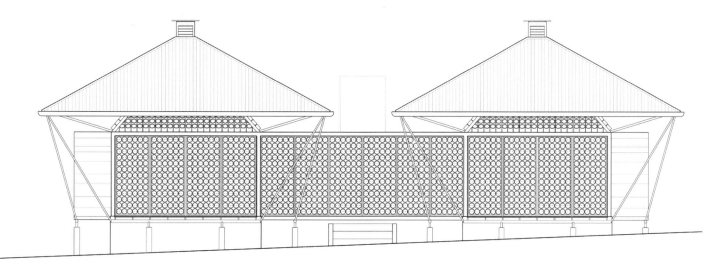

Frontal elevation

Section

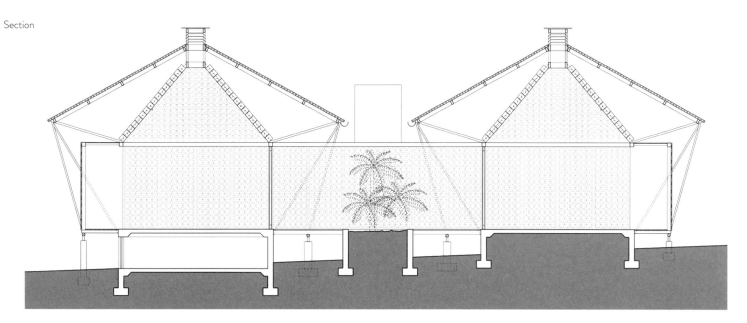

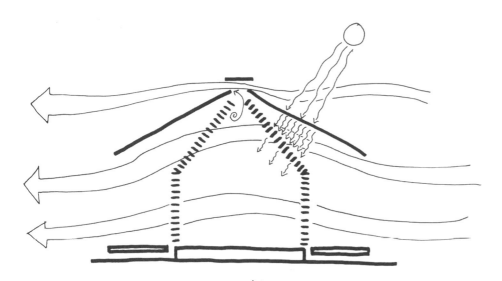

Diagram

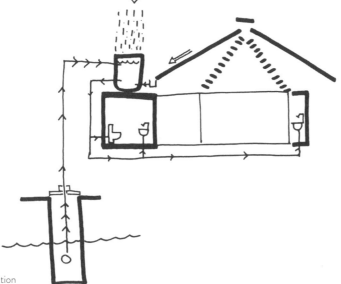

Diagram of water collection

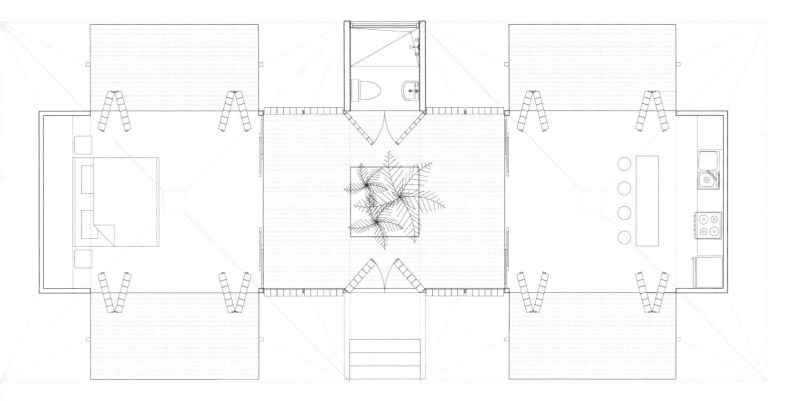

Floor layout

HILL END ECOHOUSE

RIDDEL ARCHITECTURE, ROBERT RIDDEL
Design architects: Emma Scragg & David Gole
Location: Queensland, Australia
Photos: © Christopher Frederick Jones

North east axonometric

1. Operable sunshading blind.
2. Ventilated wall cavities with recycled hardwood stud frame.
3. Solar hot water.
4. Local plantation timber joinery throughout.
5. Overhang sized for winter sun & summer shade throughout.
6. Photovoltaic panels.
7. Sunshading trellis with deciduous vines.
8. Recycled content concrete.
9. Edible landscaping throughout.
10. 25000 L of rainwater storage for pool & garden.
11. Pond for summer cooling & habitat.
12. Greywater treatment plant.
13. 45000 L of rainwater storage for house.

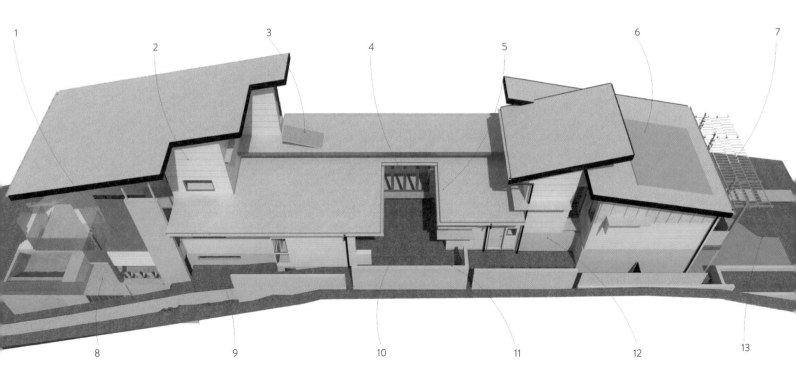

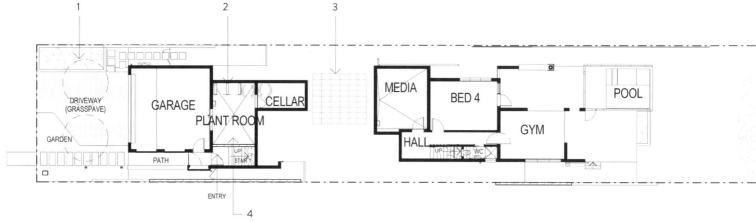

Ground floor plan
1. 45,000 L Underground rainwater tanks. Household supply.
2. Grey water treatment (irrigation, toilets, washing machine).
3. 25,000 L Permeable underground water storage. Irrigation and pool.
4. Solar power invertor, rainwater pumps and water filters.

Main floor plan
1. Tank pre-filter unit.
2. 25,000 L rainwater storage below.
3. Light slot to lower floor.

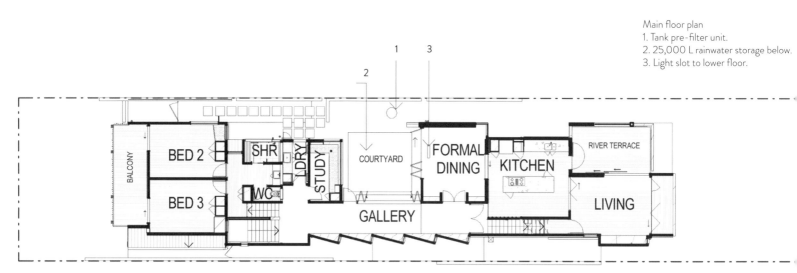

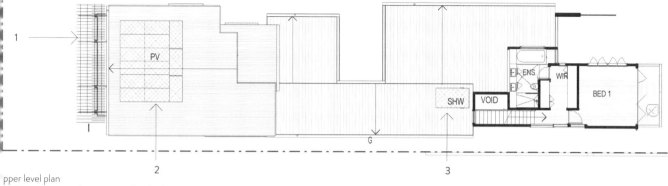

pper level plan
Trellis structure with vegetation for shading.
3.2kW solar array.
Solar hot water unit.

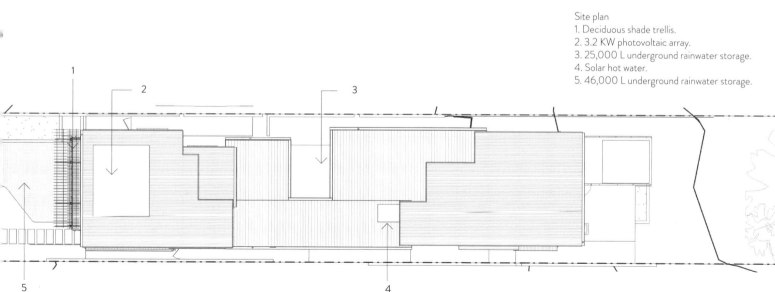

Site plan
1. Deciduous shade trellis.
2. 3.2 KW photovoltaic array.
3. 25,000 L underground rainwater storage.
4. Solar hot water.
5. 46,000 L underground rainwater storage.

East elevation
1. Retractable sunshading screen.
2. Garden bed.

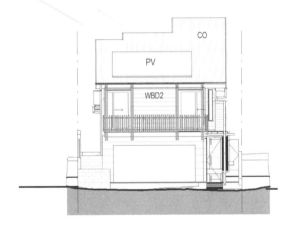

North elevation

South elevation

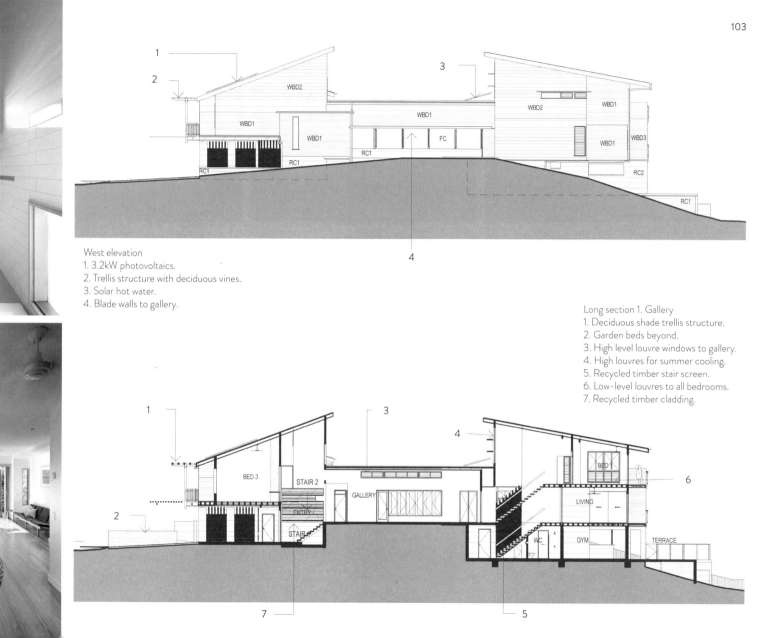

West elevation
1. 3.2kW photovoltaics.
2. Trellis structure with deciduous vines.
3. Solar hot water.
4. Blade walls to gallery.

Long section 1. Gallery
1. Deciduous shade trellis structure.
2. Garden beds beyond.
3. High level louvre windows to gallery.
4. High louvres for summer cooling.
5. Recycled timber stair screen.
6. Low-level louvres to all bedrooms.
7. Recycled timber cladding.

GULLY HOUSE

SHANE THOMPSON / BLIGH VOLLER NIELD, DANIEL FOX
Location: Brisbane, Queensland, Australia
Photos: © David Sandison
www.shanethompson.com.au

Site plan

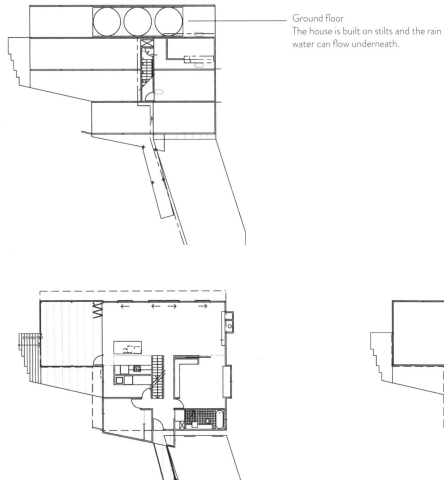

Ground floor
The house is built on stilts and the rain
water can flow underneath.

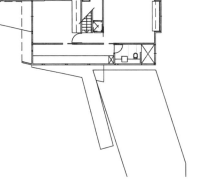

First floor

Second floor

JOANOPOLIS HOUSE

UNA ARQUITECTOS

Location: Joanopolis, Brazil

Photos: © Bebete Viégas

www.unabv.com.br

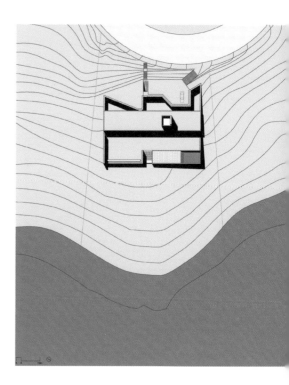

Site plan

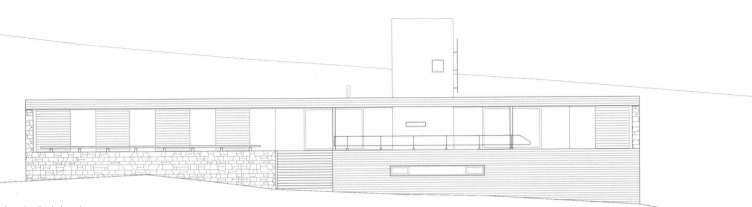

Longitudinal elevation
Elements for natural insulation: a green roof, gravel in the courtyard, etc.

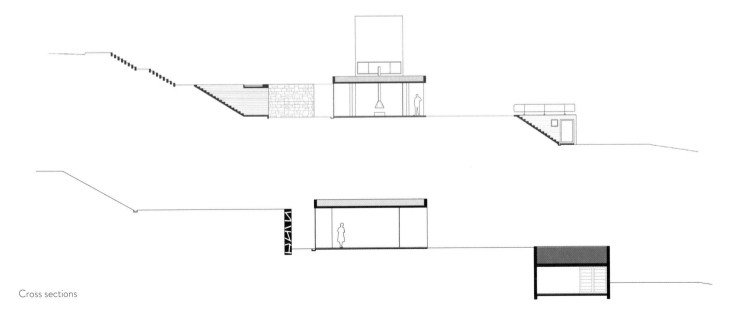

Cross sections

0 1   5m

Top floor
Rainwater collection

PASSIVE HOUSE V.W.

FRANKLIN AZZI ARCHITECTURE

Location: Normandy, France

Photos: © Franklin Azzi Architecture, Emmanuelle Blanc

www.franklinazzi.fr

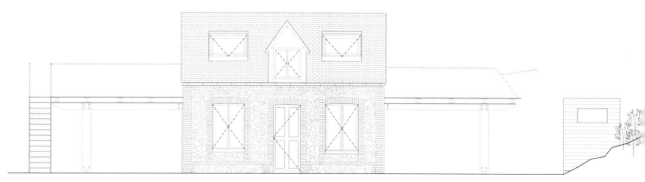

East-west section

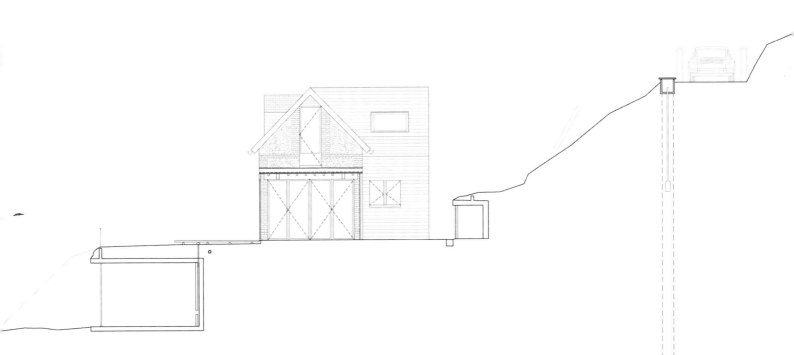

North-south section through site.
Rainwater harvesting to meet non-potable water needs. A 80-meter-deep well supplies drinking water.
Hot water and heating are obtained by means of a combination of hybrid solar and geothermal systems.

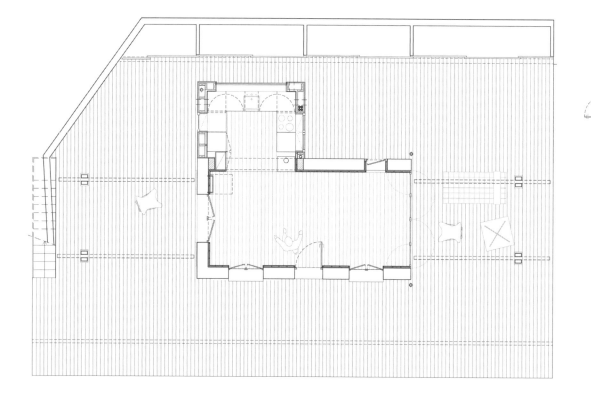

Ground floor plan

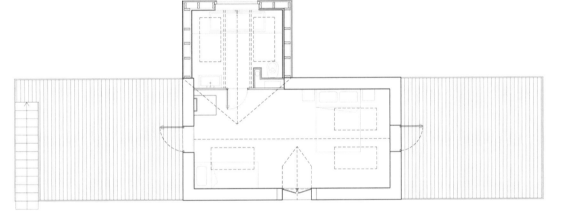

Second floor plan

VILLA NUOTA

TUOMO SIITONEN ARCHITECTS
Location: Kerimäki, Finland
Photos: © Rauno Träskelin, Mikko Auerniittyy
www.tsi.fi

Site plan

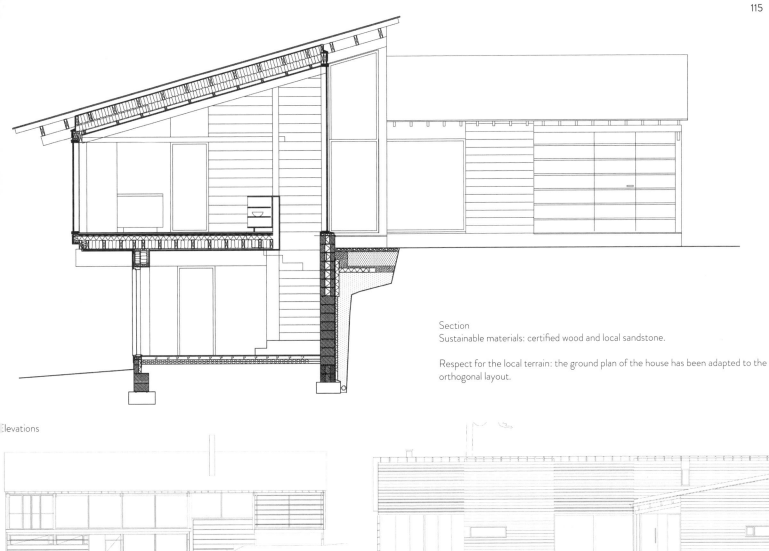

Section
Sustainable materials: certified wood and local sandstone.

Respect for the local terrain: the ground plan of the house has been adapted to the orthogonal layout.

Elevations

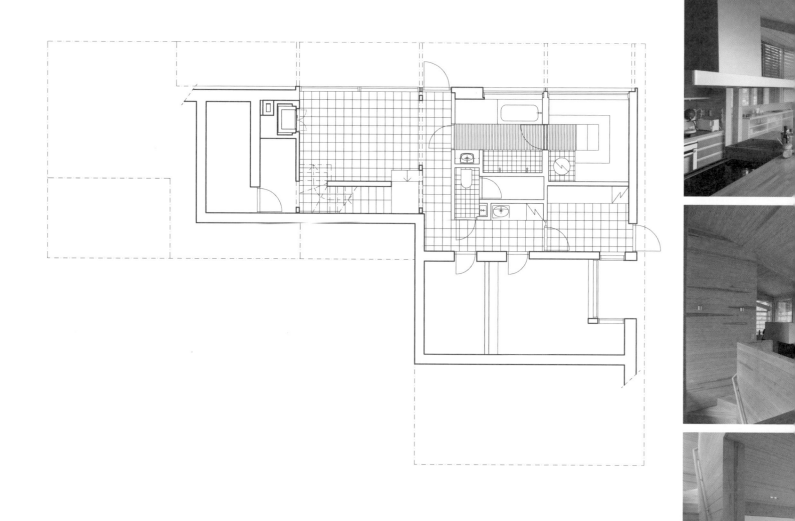

Ground floor

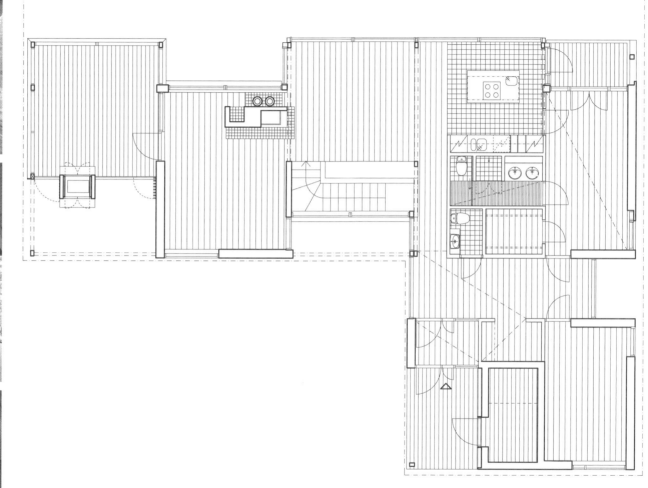

First floor

IT HOUSE

TAALMAN KOCH ARCHITECTS

Location: California, USA

Photos: © Art Gray

www.taalmanarchitecture.com

Site plan

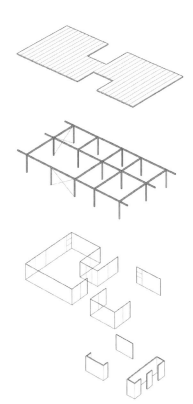

Axonometric view

Despite this property's large glazed areas, high energy efficiency is achieved through passive conditioning, in other words, the direction the house is facing, the cross ventilation, the low consumption equipment and the solar panels. These panels are incorporated into the house design and positioned over the central patio to provide shade in summer. In the winter these same panels provide the necessary energy for the electricity and the radiant floor heating.

In winter the house is heated by a radiant floor heating system which works off solar energy and wood stoves. In summer the house is cooled by external shades, curtains and a passive cooling system.

A'BODEGA

ESTEL ORTEGA VÁZQUEZ + DAVID POU VAN DEN BOSSCHE

Location: Doade, Lugo, Spain
Photos: © Adrià Goula

Site plan

Roof floor

First floor

Ground floor

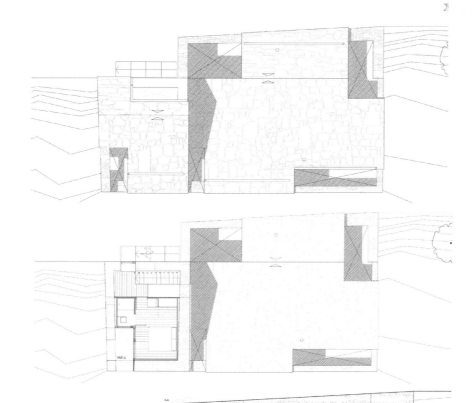

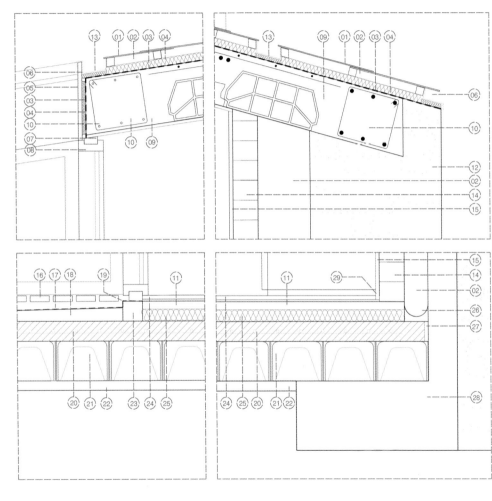

1. Waterproof roof in irregular old slate. First course.
2. Ventilation air chamber.
3. Waterproofing.
4. Thermal insulation with extruded polystyrene.
5. Wooden protection slab linings. 20x20 mm strips.
6. Metallic perimeter skirting.
7. Tubular pre-frame. 70x20x30 mm.
8. Exterior carpentry. See details.
9. Beam and panel structure.
10. Reinforced concrete ring beam. Depending on structural detail.
11. Layer of mortar.
12. Exposed stone wall.
13. Plated guttering.
14. Ceramic wall.
15. Plastering and paintwork.
16. Raised wooden platform, treated for external use.
17. Terrace asphalt cloth, with raised perimeter skirting.
18. Slope with concrete.
19. Perimeter sealing with Sikaflex.
20. 10 cm concrete flooring with 20x20 cm/6 mm diameter mesh reinforcement.
21. Ventilated drainage structure with plastic cavities.
22. Lean concrete levelling layer for cavity placement.
23. Construction support base for pre-frame and carpentry.
24. Treated oak chestnut flooring.
25. Thermal insulation.
26. Drainage guttering on existing stone wall.
27. 2 cm porexpan perimeter join for expansion.
28. Reinforced concrete wall and pad.
29. Delivery of flooring/partitions for perimeter base resolution.

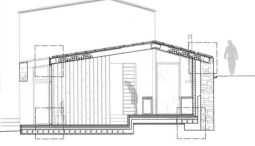

Cross sections

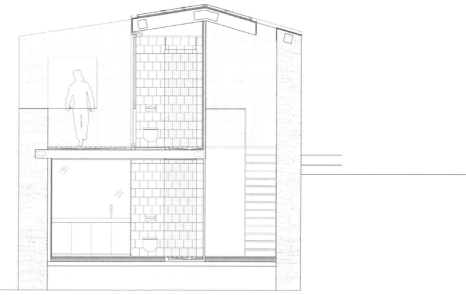

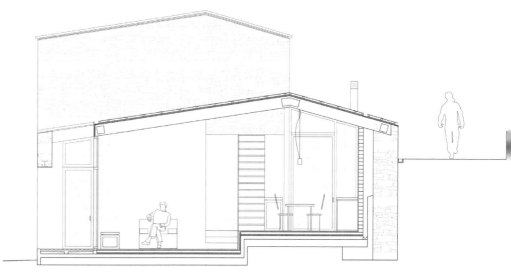

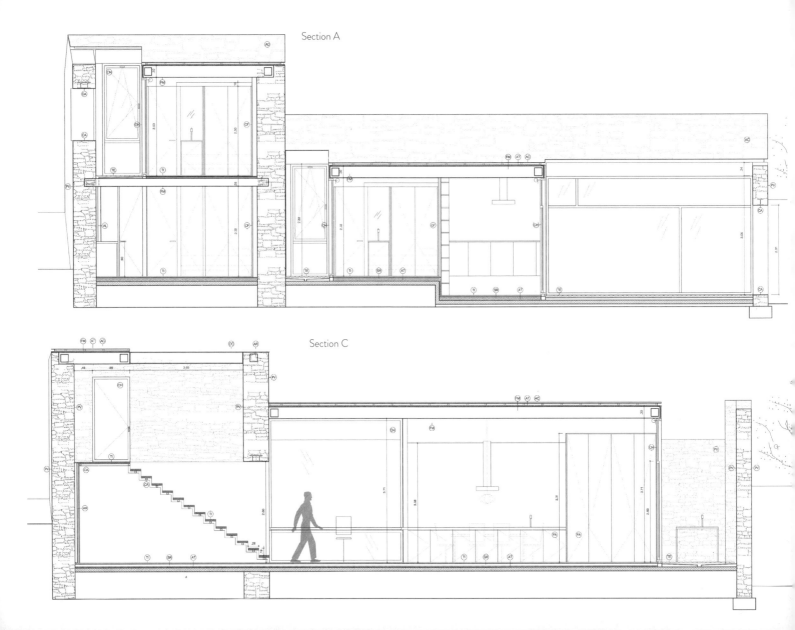

Section A

Section C

CASA TMOLO

PYO ARQUITECTOS

Ophélie Herranz Lespagnol, Paul Galindo Pastre
Location: Asturias, Spain
Photos: © Miguel de Guzmán / Imagen Subliminal
www.pyoarquitectos.com

Site plan

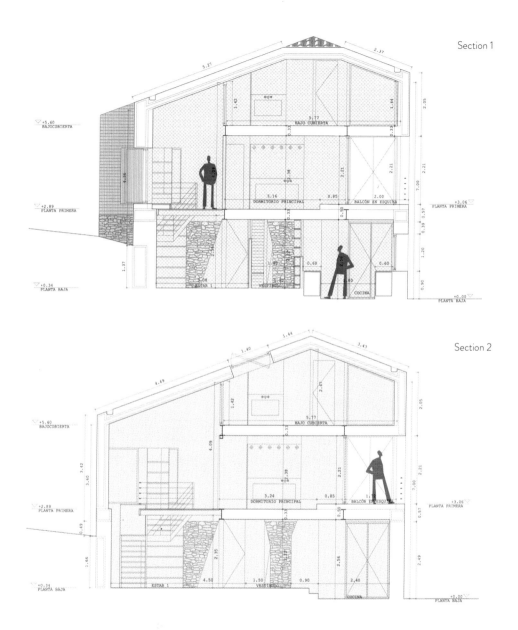

Section 1

Section 2

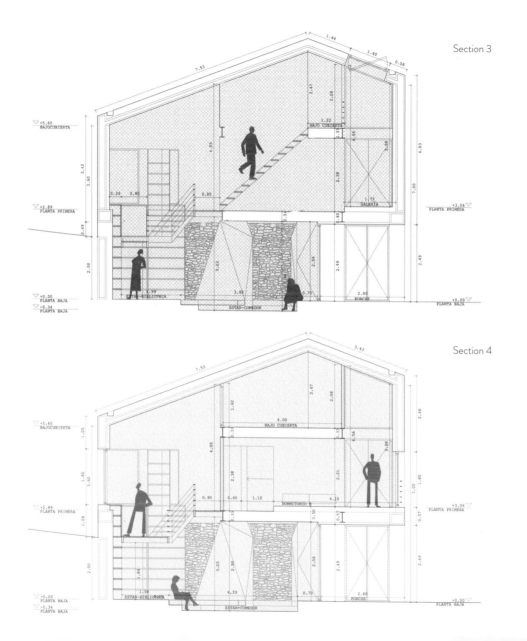

Section 3

Section 4

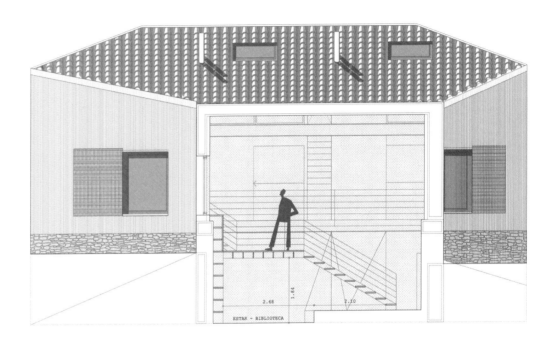

ESTAR - BIBLIOTECA

2.68   1.84   2.10

Section 5
A mix of white concrete and iron beams coexist with well-worn
stone, weather-beaten wood and local stone.

Section ground floor

Ground floor

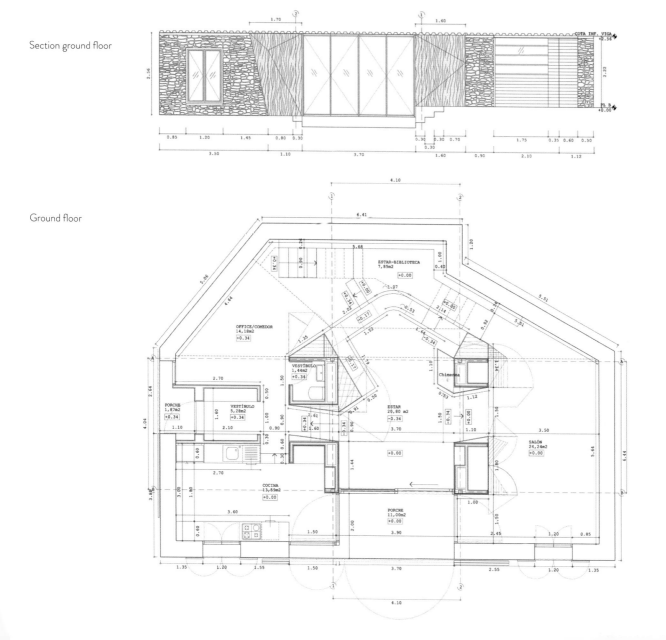

Section ground floor

First floor

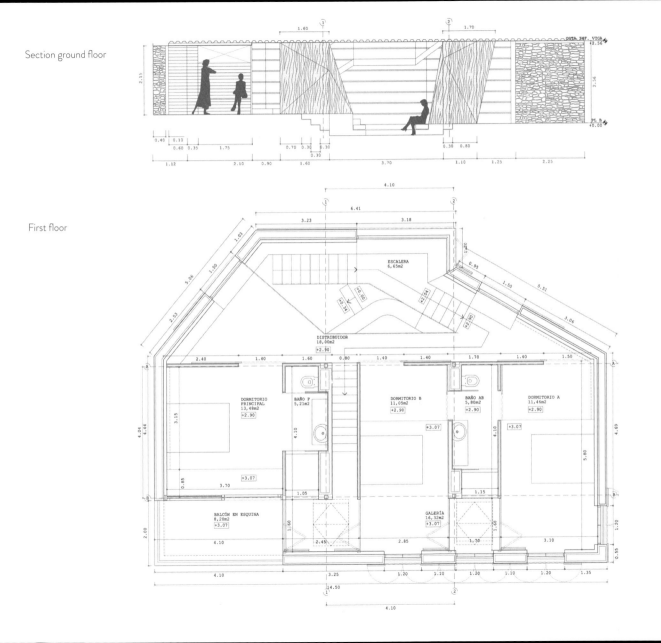

Axonometric section
The interior space is organized around four
diamond-shaped elements which run vertically
through the house

In the interior, supporting walls were replaced by
light metal pillars, opening up a large triple-height
living room along the entire length of the building,
which allows daylight to enter.

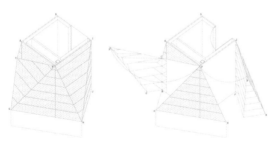

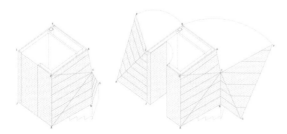

GREEN.O.LA

WORKSHOP/APD

Location: New Orleans, LA, USA

Photos: © Max Kim-Bee, T.G. Olcott

www.workshopapd.com

3D image

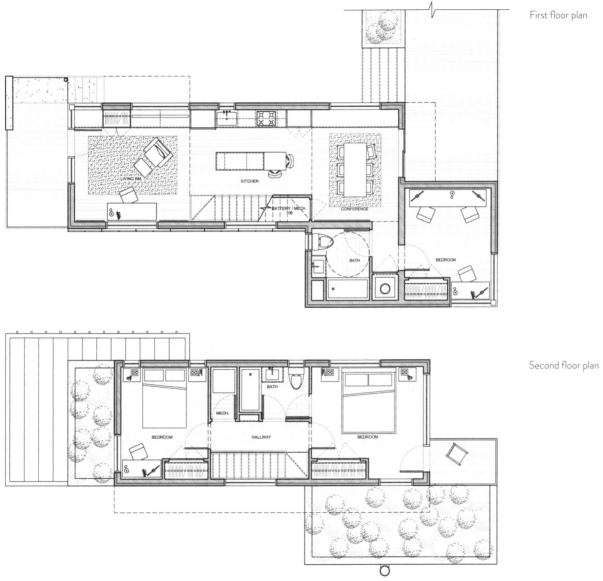

LIVING RM.

KITCHEN

BATTERY / MECH.
106

CONFERENCE

BATH

BEDROOM

Second floor plan

BEDROOM

MECH.

BATH

HALLWAY

BEDROOM

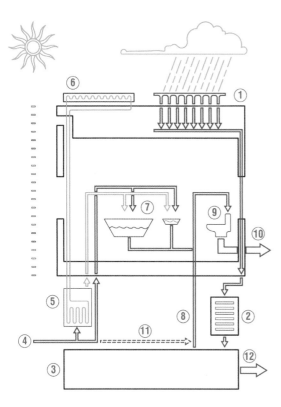

WATER SYSTEMS

1. RAIN WATER COLLECTION
2. FILTER SYSTEM
3. WATER CISTERN
4. MUNICIPAL WATER SUPPLY
5. HOT WATER STORAGE TANK
6. SOLAR WATER HEATERS
7. DOMESTIC FIXTURES
8. CISTERN SUPPLY
9. TOILETS
10. BLACK WATER DISCHARGE TO SEWER
11. AUXILIARY SUPPLY
12. TO MECHANICAL SYSTEM

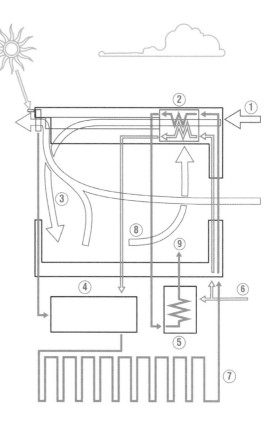

HEATING/COOLING

1. MECHANICAL FRESH AIR INTAKE
2. HEAT PUMP
3. DEHUMIDIFIER
4. WATER STORAGE CISTERN
5. WATER HEATER
6. MUNICIPAL WATER SUPPLY
7. GEOTHERMAL LOOP
8. FRESH AIR RETURN
9. UNIT HOT WATER SUPPLY

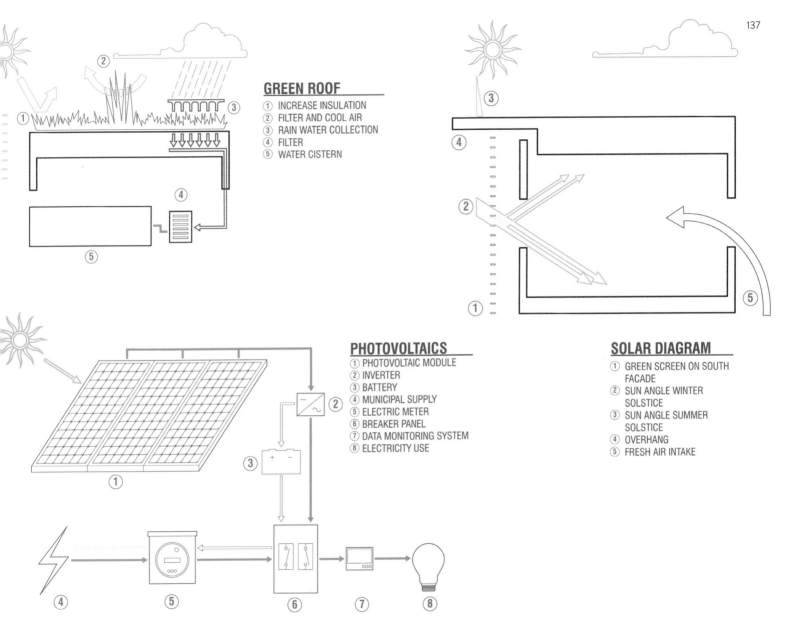

GREEN ROOF
① INCREASE INSULATION
② FILTER AND COOL AIR
③ RAIN WATER COLLECTION
④ FILTER
⑤ WATER CISTERN

PHOTOVOLTAICS
① PHOTOVOLTAIC MODULE
② INVERTER
③ BATTERY
④ MUNICIPAL SUPPLY
⑤ ELECTRIC METER
⑥ BREAKER PANEL
⑦ DATA MONITORING SYSTEM
⑧ ELECTRICITY USE

SOLAR DIAGRAM
① GREEN SCREEN ON SOUTH FACADE
② SUN ANGLE WINTER SOLSTICE
③ SUN ANGLE SUMMER SOLSTICE
④ OVERHANG
⑤ FRESH AIR INTAKE

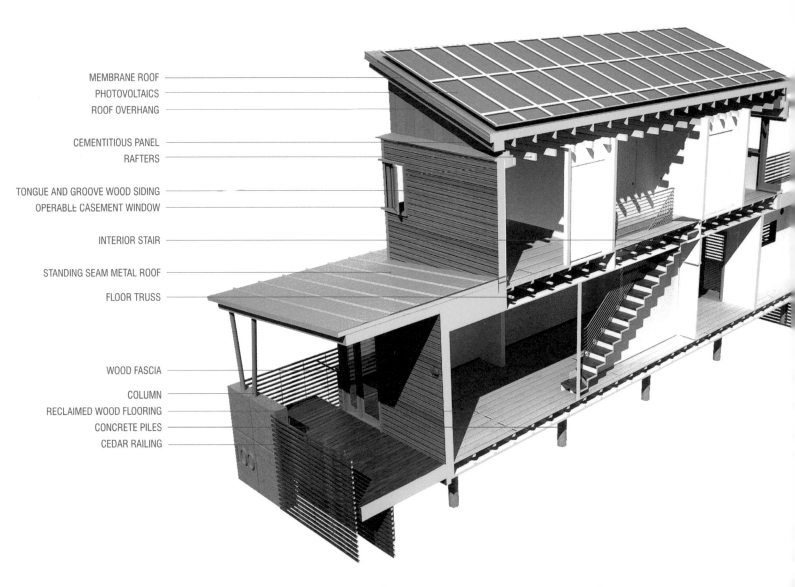

MEMBRANE ROOF

PHOTOVOLTAICS

ROOF OVERHANG

CEMENTITIOUS PANEL

RAFTERS

TONGUE AND GROOVE WOOD SIDING

OPERABLE CASEMENT WINDOW

INTERIOR STAIR

STANDING SEAM METAL ROOF

FLOOR TRUSS

WOOD FASCIA

COLUMN

RECLAIMED WOOD FLOORING

CONCRETE PILES

CEDAR RAILING

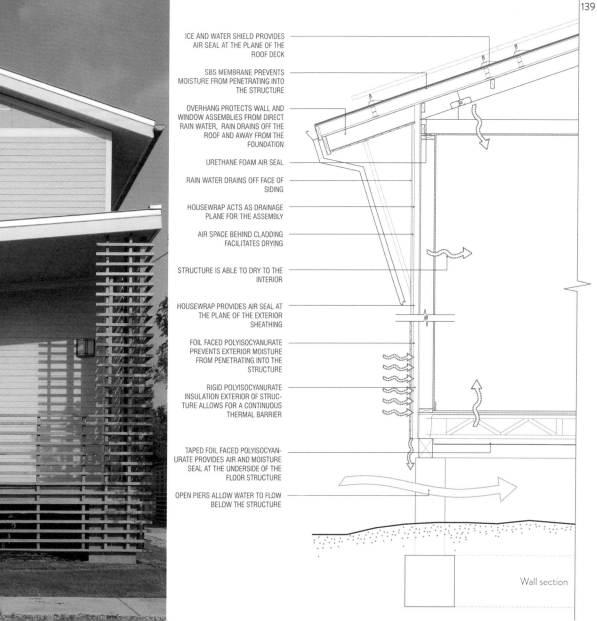

ICE AND WATER SHIELD PROVIDES AIR SEAL AT THE PLANE OF THE ROOF DECK

SBS MEMBRANE PREVENTS MOISTURE FROM PENETRATING INTO THE STRUCTURE

OVERHANG PROTECTS WALL AND WINDOW ASSEMBLIES FROM DIRECT RAIN WATER, RAIN DRAINS OFF THE ROOF AND AWAY FROM THE FOUNDATION

URETHANE FOAM AIR SEAL

RAIN WATER DRAINS OFF FACE OF SIDING

HOUSEWRAP ACTS AS DRAINAGE PLANE FOR THE ASSEMBLY

AIR SPACE BEHIND CLADDING FACILITATES DRYING

STRUCTURE IS ABLE TO DRY TO THE INTERIOR

HOUSEWRAP PROVIDES AIR SEAL AT THE PLANE OF THE EXTERIOR SHEATHING

FOIL FACED POLYISOCYANURATE PREVENTS EXTERIOR MOISTURE FROM PENETRATING INTO THE STRUCTURE

RIGID POLYISOCYANURATE INSULATION EXTERIOR OF STRUC-TURE ALLOWS FOR A CONTINUOUS THERMAL BARRIER

TAPED FOIL FACED POLYISOCYAN-URATE PROVIDES AIR AND MOISTURE SEAL AT THE UNDERSIDE OF THE FLOOR STRUCTURE

OPEN PIERS ALLOW WATER TO FLOW BELOW THE STRUCTURE

Wall section

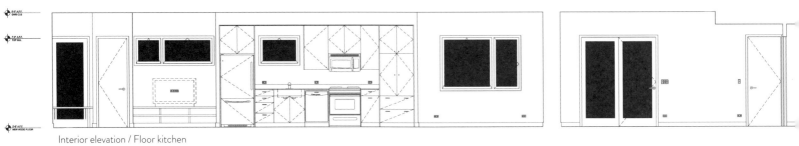

Interior elevation / Floor kitchen

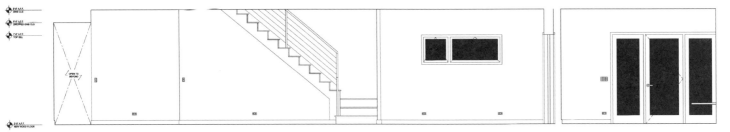

Interior elevation / Floor stair

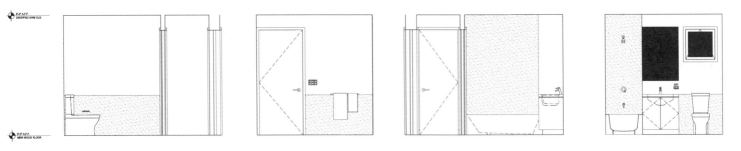

Interior elevation / Bathroom

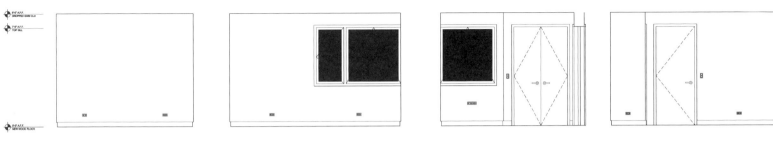

Interior elevation / Bedroom

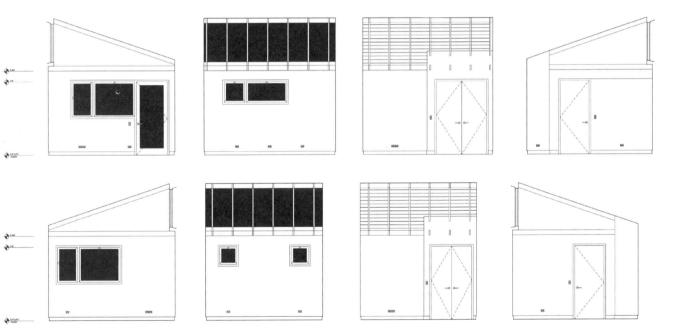

Interior elevation / Master bedroom

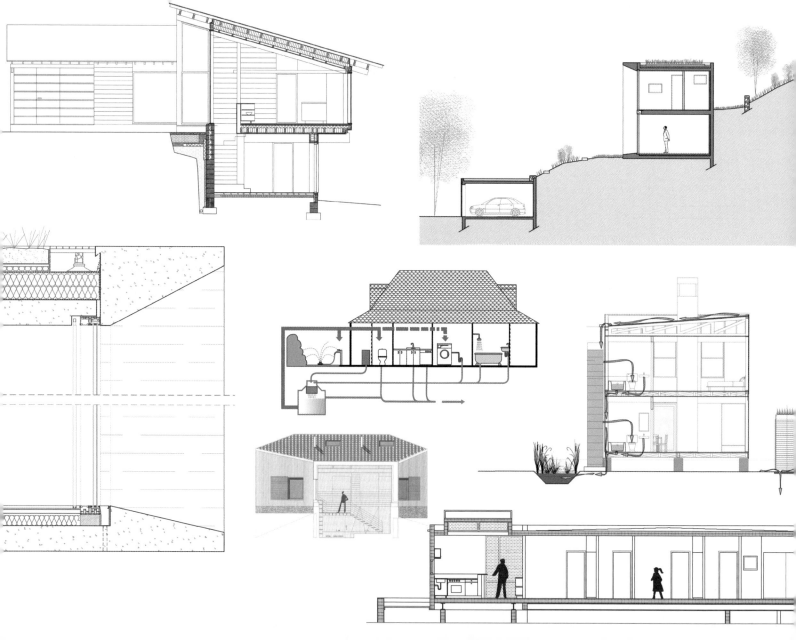